Application Cases
in
MIS

Fifth Edition

James Morgan
Northern Arizona University

McGraw-Hill Irwin

Boston   Burr Ridge, IL   Dubuque, IA   Madison, WI   New York   San Francisco   St. Louis
Bangkok   Bogotá   Caracas   Kuala Lumpur   Lisbon   London   Madrid   Mexico City
Milan   Montreal   New Delhi   Santiago   Seoul   Singapore   Sydney   Taipei   Toronto

McGraw-Hill
Irwin

APPLICATION CASES IN MIS
James Morgan

Published by McGraw-Hill/Irwin, an imprint of The McGraw-Hill Companies, Inc., 1221 Avenue of the Americas, New York, NY 10020. Copyright © 2005, 2002, 1999, 1996, 1993 by The McGraw-Hill Companies, Inc. All rights reserved.

1 2 3 4 5 6 7 8 9 0 QPD/QPD 0 9 8 7 6 5 4

ISBN 0-07-293363-1

Editorial director: *Rob Zwettler*
Publisher: *Stewart Mattson*
Sponsoring editor: *Paul Ducham*
Developmental editor: *Jennifer Wisnowski*
Marketing manager: *Douglas Reiner*
Media producer: *Greg Bates*
Production supervisor: *Gina Hangos*
Designer: *Mary Kazak*
Supplement producer: *Lynn M. Bluhm*

www.mhhe.com

TABLE OF CONTENTS

CHAPTER 4: SPREADSHEET CASES

CHAPTER 5: DEVELOPING DATABASE APPLICATIONS

CHAPTER 6: DATABASE CASES

PREFACE

Application Cases in MIS was written to support any MIS textbook that is used for courses with a substantial hands-on component. This casebook is designed to assist students in learning to design and develop hands-on computer applications to solve managerial problems. It is written for students who are prospective managerial users of computer systems, and not for potential information systems professionals. The cases presented in this casebook are business oriented. However, the methods and skills covered here should be useful to anyone working in a managerial level professional capacity in any type of organization.

The primary goal of this casebook is to help students learn to design and develop computer applications, which use common end user software packages to solve real world managerial problems. The cases presented here are centered on combinations of Internet skills, spreadsheet skills, and database management skills.

There are no cases in this book centered on work with word processing or presentation software packages, however the assigned work for nearly all of the cases requires students to "incorporate" selected results of, their application in a memorandum or report or into a "set of slides" for a business presentation. In those instances, students are expected to use a word processing package or use Power Point or a similar presentation package to complete the assignment. Many of the cases include assignments requiring the student to prepare a set of business presentation materials, e.g., Power Point slides. To build presentation skills, instructors may combine these assignments with a requirement to present the results of a case one or more times over the semester.

This casebook is designed for use in classes where incoming students are expected to have some prior experience with the use of spreadsheet and database packages and with the word processing and presentation software needed to complete the case assignments. Thus, the mechanics of using software packages are not covered in this casebook. However, only a minimal level of knowledge of these packages is required to complete the cases presented here. Similarly, it is assumed that students have had some experience with information retrieval through the Internet or that they can learn these skills through on-line help.

Students without previous experience in the use of these common business application packages, and students who feel that they need to refresh their skills in the use of these packages may need to use supplemental materials such as reference manuals or tutorial workbooks to develop the fundamental skills needed to complete these cases. One such resource is the Simnet MIS tutorial CD, available from McGraw-Hill, which provides interactive tutorials covering a variety of spreadsheet and database skills.

To help instructors and students identify the business and computer application skills needed to complete each case, a Case Skills Matrix is provided immediately following this preface. This Case Skills Matrix describes the business topic skills covered by the case (listed in italics) and then summarizes the software skills needed to complete each case.

Students enter MIS courses with widely varied levels of experience in the other functional areas of business. The cases presented in this casebook have been designed to present real world business situations without requiring the use of advanced functional area skills that some students may not have. Brief explanations are provided when basic terminology or calculations requiring on functional area knowledge are used.

Building end user applications requires more than simply having a technical knowledge of spreadsheet and database packages. The end user developer must be able to identify situations calling for the development of an end user computer application and must be able to design and develop an application that will provide the appropriate information in as effective a manner as possible. These skills in identifying problem situations requiring computer applications and designing solutions are key to successful use of computer technology, and form the main thrust of this casebook.

Three sets of cases are presented: a set of applications using the Internet, a set of spreadsheet applications, and a set of database applications. Some of the database cases require the integrated use of both database and spreadsheet software and several of the spreadsheet and database cases involve incorporating information gathered from the Internet into spreadsheets or database tables.

A chapter of material describing applicable design and development tools and methods and applying them to a sample case is presented before each set of cases. The chapter materials describing development tools and methods assume the use of a windows environment with integrated application packages and an available Internet browser. The cases present real world problem situations in a narrative form. Application designs are presented for the first four cases in the spreadsheet and database chapters to help give students a better feel for the design process. However, the remaining cases in each set require the student to design and develop an appropriate application based only upon the narrative problem description.

The windows based "suites" of application development software packages have simplified the process of building applications that use multiple tools (e.g. spreadsheet, database, word processing, and presentation software) in an integrated fashion. The ability to use these packages effectively in an integrated fashion is an important skill and is emphasized in the cases of this edition.

The web site for this casebook provides startup files for use on those cases requiring the use of substantial amounts of data. These files are provided in order to reduce the amount of repetitive data entry required to complete these cases. Completed files for the sample cases presented in Chapters 1, 3, and 5 are also available for download. The files for spreadsheet cases are in EXCEL format and those for database case in ACCESS format, but they should be readable by most common commercial spreadsheet and database packages. The requirements for your computer system to be able to support the cases in this book are quite minimal.

These files will have the names indicated in this casebook and can be found at the Internet site:

http:/www.mhhe.com/business/mis/morgan/5ed.

System Requirements

In order to use this casebook effectively, students must have access to:

1. Spreadsheet software that can read files created by EXCEL.
2. Database software that can read or convert files created by ACCESS.
3. Word processing software and (ideally) business presentation software.
4. Internet browser software.
5. A computer system with enough memory to operate the software listed above.

Assessing Skills Required

To help instructors and students identify the business and computer application skills needed to complete each case, a Case Skills Matrix is provided immediately following this preface. This Case Skills Matrix describes the business topic skills covered by the case (listed in italics) and then summarizes the software skills needed to complete each case. Also included, for those who have purchased the Simnet MIS CD, is a table suggesting tutorials that might be used to review many of the needed spreadsheet and database skills.

CASE SKILLS MATRIX

Chapter 2: Internet Cases

Case	Skills Required
All	Basic Word Processing (to write up reports and memoranda)
1.	*Internet information retrieval*
	Basic PowerPoint skills (or similar presentation software) Assignment 1
	Basic Spreadsheet skills (optional)
2.	*Internet information retrieval*
	Basic PowerPoint skills (or similar presentation software) Assignment 1
3.	*Internet information retrieval*
	Basic PowerPoint skills (or similar presentation software) Assignment 2
	Basic Spreadsheet skills
4.	*Internet information retrieval and analysis*
	Basic PowerPoint skills (or similar presentation software) Assignment 2
5.	*Internet information retrieval and analysis*
	Basic Spreadsheet skills
6.	*Internet information retrieval and analysis*
	Basic PowerPoint skills (or similar presentation software) Assignment 2
7.	Basic Web Page creation skills
8.	Basic Web Page creation skills
9.	Basic Web Page creation skills

Chapter 4: Spreadsheet Cases

Case	Skills Required
All	Basic Spreadsheet skills
	Basic Word Processing (to write up reports and memoranda)
1.	*Actual versus Budgeted Expenditures*
	Basic PowerPoint skills (or similar presentation software) Assignment 3
2.	*Income statement Trend Analysis*
	Graph/chart creation skills
	Internet information retrieval skills Assignment 3
	Basic PowerPoint skills (or similar presentation software) Assignment 4
3.	*Sales Performance Analysis – Exception Reporting*
	Graph/chart creation skills
	Basic PowerPoint skills (or similar presentation software) Assignment 3
4.	*Business startup profitability analysis*
	Basic PowerPoint skills (or similar presentation software) Assignment 3
5.	*Personnel Expense Trend Analysis*
	Graph/chart creation skills
	Basic Web Page creation skills Assignment 3
	Export of Spreadsheet to a web page Assignment 3
6.	*Sales Performance Bonus Analysis*
7.	*Income and Balance Sheet Common Size Analysis*
	Internet information retrieval skills Assignment 3
8.	*Costing and Analysis of Alternatives to provide an Employee Benefit*
9.	*Analysis of Accounts Receivable Trends*
	Basic PowerPoint skills (or similar presentation software) Assignment 2

Chapter 6: Database Cases

Case	Skills Required
All	Basic database Querying and Reporting Skills
	Basic Word Processing (to write up reports and memoranda)
1.	*Human Relations*
	Database table Modification
	Basic Web Page creation skills Assignment 4
2.	*Sales performance / sales commission analysis*
	Database table Creation
	Multiple tables and relationships
	Basic PowerPoint skills (or similar presentation software) Assignment 3
3.	*Small business product sales and servicing*
	Database table Creation
	Multiple tables and relationships
	Data entry form Creation
	Basic PowerPoint skills (or similar presentation software) Assignment 2
4.	*Production quality Assurance*
	Copying query results to a spreadsheet
	Basic Spreadsheet skills
	Basic PowerPoint skills (or similar presentation software) Assignment 3
5.	*Sales analysis – sell through*
	Basic PowerPoint skills (or similar presentation software) Assignment 2
6.	*Small business sales system*
	Database table Creation
	Multiple tables and relationships
	Data entry form Creation
7.	*Human Resources – Job assignment*
	Database table Creation
	Multiple tables and relationships
	Data entry form Creation
	Basic PowerPoint skills (or similar presentation software) Assignment 2
8.	*Sales Performance Bonus Analysis*
	Basic PowerPoint skills (or similar presentation software) Assignment 2
9.	*Production quality Assurance*
	Database table Creation

Spreadsheet and Database Skills Supported by the Simnet MIS CD

Skill	Simnet MIS Tutorial Section
Spreadsheet	
Basic Spreadsheet skills	Lessons 1, 2, 3, 4-1, 4-2, and 5
Graph/chart creation skills	Lesson 6
Export of a spreadsheet to a web page	Lesson 7-1
Database	
Basic database Querying and Reporting Skills	Lessons 1, 3-1, 5-2, 5-3, 5-4, 7
Database table Creation / Modification	Lessons 2, 5-1
Multiple tables and relationships	Lesson 6
Data entry form Creation	Lesson 4

Chapter 1: BUSINESS APPLICATIONS AND THE INTERNET

Today the Internet has a wide ranging impact on the way business is conducted and on the way we live. The volume of communications and commerce handled by the Internet is growing exponentially. The impact of the Internet on organizational communications and on organizational information systems is so broad that we can only provide a few brief examples in this case book.

Users can access the internet for information retrieval and can even produce simple World Wide Web sites without having a great deal of technical knowledge of the internet and its related technologies. These types of uses of the Internet are the ones that are most important to managerial end users, and will be the focus of the Internet cases presented here.

A number of web browsers and on-line services are available which provide easy access to the World Wide Web and the Internet for information retrieval. These products and services provide a graphical interface to interact with the Internet and have lots of help if you get lost. The coverage presented here assumes that you have already used the internet for information retrieval or that you can learn on your own using the help in the browser or information service that you are using to access the internet.

In order to provide a broad overview of ways in which the Internet can be used in business applications, three distinct types of cases will be described in this chapter and present for you to complete in Chapter 2. These are:

A.   Retrieval Cases, which require retrieval of information from the internet to support a traditional application (spreadsheet or database),

B.   Web Assessment Cases, where you are asked to examine the web sites of businesses and assess the effectiveness with which this medium is being used, and

C.   Web Creation cases, which require you to create your own simple web pages.

RETRIEVAL CASES

The Internet is very commonly used as a research source in preparing business reports and presentations. Information gathered from the internet may become the input component of a spreadsheet or database application, or it may provide more qualitative information to be incorporated directly into a report or presentation. This is, perhaps, the simplest way to use the Internet in building an information systems application. We use the Internet to for information gathering to support our analysis. For example, we might gather pricing data from several companies to support a spreadsheet for a purchasing decision, corporate earning information for a stock purchase decision, or even reviews of market trends and corporate strategy to produce an assessment of a company's expected future performance. The internet information is either used directly in a report or presentation or, if appropriate, data gathered from the Internet becomes the input data for a spreadsheet or database application.

Because web technology allows anyone to express their ideas and opinions to a world-wide audience, it is particularly important that researchers evaluate their sources and seek out multiple and balanced sources when doing internet research. It is also critically important that you appropriately cite web resources that are used to support your research so that others can access those sites for further information. According to the American Psychological Association, citations of internet web page should always include the html address and the date when you accessed it, in addition to the standard citation information of the title of the item your are referencing, the author if an author is identified, and the name of the organization responsible for the web site where your reference was found.

Where a web site provides significant amounts of quantitative data that data is often provided in the form of downloadable files in a format that can be read directly by your spreadsheet or database software to provide the input data for an application. Downloading the initial data for the cases in this book is a simple example of this type of use. You can see how this works by going to the web site at **http:/www.mhhe.com/business/mis/morgan/5th**. Simply follow the instructions to download a file (the **witsdata** spreadsheet file, for instance), then retrieve the file into the appropriate software package and verify that you can use it.

The first three cases in the next chapter are primarily information retrieval cases involving no quantitative data or relatively limited amounts of quantitative data. They can be completed using only very small and basic spreadsheets and without any use of database software. Additional cases involving Internet information retrieval combined with more advanced spreadsheet or database work will be presented in later chapters. Spreadsheet and database cases that also use Internet skills will be designated by the following icon: ⊕

WEB ASSESSMENT CASES

Web assessment cases ask you to examine the use of the Internet, and particularly the World Wide Web, as a type of strategic information system. You are asked to examine web sites of existing firms to see how effectively they have used the Internet and to perform some comparative assessments. These cases may require you to create a small spreadsheet based on what you retrieve, but their focus is on the evaluation of the effectiveness of an organization's Web pages, and how they support the organization's strategic focus. Cases 4 through 6 in the next chapter have this assessment focus.

WEB PAGE CREATION CASES

The final type of case is one that requires you to actually create a web site. As with all information systems, it is important to focus first on creating an effective design and then proceed to the actual implementation of the web site.

Effective design will make other Internet users more interested in your web site and, in a business setting, may be used to provide a strategic advantage. Some broad guidelines for effective web site design will be presented in the next section. You should use these guidelines in completing the web site creation cases. You can also apply them in the cases that ask you to evaluate the web sites of existing businesses.

Transferring your design to actual web pages requires that you create one or more files in a special language called Hypertext Mark-up Language or HTML. The HTML language is not difficult, but it is at a technical level that makes it inappropriate for use by must managerial end-users. However, a number of end-user oriented software packages have been developed or modified to allow you to build a web page without having to develop a mastery of HTML. These products allow you to enter data in a comfortable familiar form, such as a word processing file, and automatically convert what is entered into an HTML file that can be placed on the Internet. For example, Microsoft Word supports the development of web pages in its word processing environment. Users can work in their familiar word processing environment to build simple web-based applications. (For the benefit of students who have no experience with creation of web pages, a brief overview of the process required to build a simple web page using Microsoft Word is available for download at the web site for this textbook.)

It should be noted that organizational web pages often involve complex elements, such as, managing interaction with the user, security controls, and animation. Building a web site to include these elements requires knowledge of HTML, the JAVA programming language, and a number of other enabling technologies. Larger organizations have full time IS staff devoted to the development and maintenance of their web presence. However, simple but effective web pages can now be developed by end-users without great technical knowledge, as we will see. Cases 7 through 9 in the next chapter require you to create simple web pages.

BASIC PRINCIPLES OF WEB PAGE DESIGN

Web pages are much less highly structured than the spreadsheet and database applications that will be covered in later chapters. There are no hard and fast rules that, if followed, will guarantee that a web page is effective. A great deal of art is involved in the design of a web site that will be effective in appealing to the set of users who are the target for a particular site. Nevertheless, there are some important factors that should be followed when constructing a web site.

Five key elements: Content, Organization, Navigation, Economy, and Security should be considered in web design. The names chosen here are arbitrary; other texts and references may use somewhat different terms. However, this classification should be sufficient to organize your thinking about web design. Also its elements spell out an acronym (CONES) which may help you to remember them. The sequencing of these elements is designed to roughly capture the sequence in which the individual elements would normally be considered. The five design elements are briefly described in Figure 1-1 below.

Figure 1-1

Web Design Factors

Content - The content of the web site must fully communicate the information you are trying to give to its users, and must capture the user's attention. It is crucial that the message of your web site is communicated in a manner that captures the user's interest. The initial screens must attract enough interest to cause the user to continue to explore the site and the remainder of the site must hold sufficient interest to encourage repeated visits. Creative use and integration of language, color, images, sound, and/or video should be employed to capture the user's attention.

Organization - The web page must be well organized with the information divided into logical categories and subcategories which allow the user to both read through the full document in a sequential manner, and selectively drill down into topics of particular interest to them.

Navigation - The web page must have an effective navigation scheme, which allows the user to move through a document sequentially, or go directly to more detailed information about a topic of interest. At any level, it should also always be possible to link directly back to the opening screen. It is also helpful to provide links to other related web pages either on your site or at other sites on the Web. These navigational links are commonly provided by specially highlighted items of text, or by buttons or icons, all of which can be clicked with the mouse to move to the indicated topic.

Economy - There should be an economy both in the number of screens that a user must traverse to get to an item of interest and in the amount of data that the site sends to the user's computer. Web pages are designed to be open to all. Modem speeds and browser capabilities limit the ability of some users to read large image files and video clips. When such items are used, it is usually best to put them in a file that is only called up if the user chooses to retrieve it.

Security - A web site that allows users to access potentially sensitive information or invites users to submit sensitive information about themselves (e.g. identifying information and/or charge card numbers), must provide strong security measures to ensure that this sensitive information is not compromised. All web sites must have security measures sufficient to ensure that the web site does not provide a means for hackers to access other organizational data. Passwords, encryption, and firewalls are among the forms of security commonly associated with web sites.

Content is the most crucial element of any web design. High quality content that is designed to generate and hold the user's attention is needed. An organization's "home page" becomes its first point of contact with potential customers, employees, and investors. The benefit of capturing interest and creating a professional image here should be obvious. Capturing the interest of the user is equally important in other types of web pages, such as, a personnel department's listing of job openings, safety bulletins, and benefits regulations posted on the internal "Intranet" of an organization. The budget may be lower and the challenge greater, but the goal is the same - capture the user's attention so that they will look at and remember the information you are conveying. Once you have captured the user's attention you must be sure that your site fully communicates the information users need in a manner that allows them to choose the amount of information they want without being forced to page through information that is not of interest to them.

Unfortunately, there are sometimes trade-offs between the goal of capturing attention and some of the other design elements. While creative use of color and images captures attention, inconsistent use of these elements can add confusion and make navigation of a web site more difficult. Color, size, and location standards, and standardization of icons or other images used for navigation of a web page, make it much easier to navigate a web site. This type of standardization does not substantially interfere with creative web page design.

There is a more serious trade-off with the economy element. Large detailed graphic images and video clips can substantially enhance the ability of a web page to capture the user's attention and convey information. At the same time, extensive use of these features is expensive in terms of the amount of data that must be sent to the user's computer. A dynamic video clip may captivate a user with a high-speed network connection to your site and a state-of-the-art computer system. These same features will turn-off a user with a low speed modem who must wait, perhaps for minutes, for the transfer of data that their browser may be unable to display.

A good compromise is to provide limited, but representative, images and perhaps short video clips on the home page. This should give users a feel for the visual elements of your site, without causing excessive delays for users with less capable systems. Additional graphics and longer video clips are then made available if the user clicks on an appropriate link. Links to resource intensive files should be identified in a way that will alert the user to the fact that some delay may be experienced.

This trade-off is a crucial one. It is possible to design a web site that can only serve as a toy for computer "techies" who might not even be a part of the target market for your web site. At the same time, excessive restrictions on the use of resource intensive elements can significantly reduce the effectiveness of your web page. Also, the level of data that can be incorporated in a web page without overwhelming older systems is constantly increasing, as hardware, software, and networking resources are upgraded over time. Appropriate decisions in this area require that you understand the target market for the web pages that you are developing - understand the types of computing resources they have and the level of sophistication they display in using them.

The organizational structure of web pages is often complex. What the user views as one web "site" typically consists of a number of linked files. Links can move a user to another location within the same file, or can transfer the user to another related file. The organization of a web site is basically a hierarchical one. High-level pages serve as switchboards, allowing the user to transfer to any of several more detailed pages. However, each web page may contain multiple levels of detail along with navigational links that allow users to quickly move to various sections within that one web page.

Theoretically, a web application of any degree of complexity could be placed in a single file containing as many links as needed to support navigation. However, this would make for a cumbersome web site that would be difficult to manage effectively, and would require all users to download this potentially huge document.

Typically, each individual file or page in a web application incorporates no more than two levels of detail. In a two level page, the portion of the page that appears on the screen when it pops up contains a brief discussion of the topic that is to be addressed and an outline of the sub-topics addressed in this web page. These outline items also serve as links to the point in the file where each sub-topic is addressed. Of course, some of this information, including possibly the links to sub-topics, might be presented in graphic form to stimulate interest. Following this introductory screen, the details of the sub-topic information are presented in logical order. By scrolling through the document, the user is able to efficiently read the entire document in logical order. At the same time, the user who is interested only in a selected topic, can quickly move to the detailed information about that topic. Figure 1-2 illustrates this structure.

Figure 1-2
Links Within and Between Web Page Files

Document A
Xxxxxx xxxxxxx xxx xxxxxx Xxxxxx
Xxxxxxx xxxxxx. (Introductory text
And graphics)
Subtopic 1

Subtopic 2

Subtopic 3

Subtopic 4

_____

Subtopic 1
Xxxxx xxxxxx xxxxx xxx xxxxx xxx
Xxxxxxxxx xxxx xx x xxxxxx xxxx
(details of subtopic 1)
Top of Document   Switch to Doc. B
Subtopic 2
Xxxxx xxxxxx xxxxx xxx xxxxx xxx
Xxxxxxxxx xxxx xx x xxxxxx xxxx
(details of subtopic 2)
Top of Document   Switch to Doc. C
Subtopic 3
Xxxxx xxxxxx xxxxx xxx xxxxx xxx
Xxxxxxxxx xxxx xx x xxxxxx xxxx
(details of subtopic 3)
Top of Document   Switch to Doc. D
Subtopic 4
Xxxxx xxxxxx xxxxx xxx xxxxx xxx
Xxxxxxxxx xxxx xx x xxxxxx xxxx
(details of subtopic 4)
Top of Document   Switch to Doc. E

Document B
Xxxxxx xxxxxxx xxx xxxxxx Xxxxxx
Xxxxxxx xxxxxx.
Subtopic B1

Subtopic B2

Subtopic B3

Subtopic B4

_____

Subtopic B1
Xxxxx xxxxxx xxxxx xxx xxxxx xxx
Xxxxxxxxx xxxx xx x xxxxxx xxxx
(details of subtopic B1)
Return to Site Home Page
 Return to Top of this Document
Switch to More detailed Doc (if needed)

Document C

(similar to Document B above)

Document D

(similar to Document B above)

Document E

(similar to Document B above)

For a large or complex web site, it may be necessary to have substantially more than two levels of hierarchical detail. This can be accommodated by linking the sub-topic level items of one file to another web page, which contains still more detailed information and can, if necessary, link to still more detailed pages. The linkages from page A to pages B, C, D, and E in Figure 1-2 illustrate this idea. The underlined items in Figure 1-2 represent text items that are links to other locations. From the initial viewing area of each page you can always link down to the more detailed subtopics. From the most detailed entries on any page you can always link back to the top of the page (and back to the home page if appropriate). If there is further detail or related information on another web page file, there is also a link to that related file. It should be noted that web page files having only the high level, outline style information could also be used. Each link in the outline area simply links to another file. This is particularly popular for the highest level pages of large web sites encompassing many topic areas.

APPLETON APPLIANCE SERVICE DEPARTMENT

Let's create a more concrete example and use it to demonstrate some of these principles. We'll take the service department of an appliance store as our example. We want to build a Web page for the service department at Appleton Appliances. Appleton Appliances sells and services three major brands of refrigerators, stoves, and microwave ovens. The service department wishes to create a web page so that customers can look-up information about: servicing and repair prices, qualifications and experience of the service staff, home use and servicing tips for customers, and recall and warranty information about each product line Appleton Appliances services.

The basic design of this Web page is quite simple and is illustrated in Figure 1-3. We need to have an overview area of the web page that will be visible when the page is initially retrieved. This area should contain some overview information about the service department, some appropriate pictures, links to the web sites of the appliance manufacturers that Appletons services, and a short descriptive link to the three subtopics of information associated with the site. The area below that, is accessed either by scrolling or linking to a subtopic. This is the detail area of the web page and it presents information about each of the subtopics in order. At the bottom of each subtopic entry there is a link back to the top of the web page. The scope of this application is small enough that only one additional web page file on Appleton's web site is referenced. The service manager, Al Jones, maintains a web page with pictures and information about antique appliances. This web page is maintained on Appleton's site, and can be accessed from a link at the end of Al's bio. However, the recall and warranty information line on the initial screen contains links to external web sites maintained by the respective appliance manufacturers.

An example set of web pages implementing the design described above is available on the web site for this casebook in downloadable file called **webex**. For students who have no previous experience with the creation of web pages, a brief summary of techniques for building simple web pages using Microsoft Word is provided in a file called **web_site_development** available on the web site for this case book.

SUMMARY

This chapter has presented an overview of how the Internet is impacting business. Three types of cases for exploring this impact were identified: information retrieval cases, web assessment cases, and web page creation cases. Characteristics of each type of case were described. Each type of case is represented in the set of cases in Chapter 2. You will also have the opportunity to build on your Internet skills in completing a number of cases in succeeding chapters. Cases applying Internet skills will be preceded by the 🌐 symbol.

We described a set of web page design elements called CONES. This stands for content, organization, navigation, economy, and security. Web pages can be evaluated in terms of these elements. More importantly, these elements can be used to aid in the design of a new web site, as we saw when we went through the process of developing an example web site.

Figure 1-3
Appleton Appliance Service Department Web Design

Apple Facts:

Appleton electronics was founded in 1922.

Our service staff has over 60 years
   Combined experience.

We offer complete factory authorized
   repair and servicing of most brands
   of appliances.

Our Servicing and Repair Prices are the
   Best in town.

(picture of service staff at work)

visible
on initial
retrieval

Your safety, convenience and effectiveness in using your appliances is always our concern:
   Click here for our service staff's Home Servicing and Safety Tips.

Click on a link below to retrieve a manufacturer's recall and warranty information:

   W. G., Cooking-Aid, Kool-Air { Links to the web sites of these companies

Service Department:
   We are proud of the experience that . . .

Picture of Al
Jones

Al Jones, our service manager has . . .

Click here to Look at Al's history of Appliances web Page

. . .

Return to Top of Document

scroll
or link to
these areas

Service and Repair Rates: (spreadsheet like table of rates with return link as above)

Home Servicing and Safety Tips: (list of descriptions and graphics with return link as above)

CHAPTER 2: INTERNET CASES

🌐 CASE 1: Industry Analysis

Select at least three firms in an industry of interest to you (or an industry assigned by your instructor). Using the web, research important trends in this industry and investigate each of your firms. Use standard web search techniques to find out about trends affecting the industry, then search for specific information about your selected firms. In addition, go to the web sites of your selected firms and examine their press releases and their recent annual reports for information about their current performance and strategy. Include quantitative data summarizing trends in stock prices and earnings per share.

Based upon this research: summarize the most important factors expected to impact the industry over the next three years, briefly describe the current market position of each of your firms, describe the strategy being followed by each firm, assess the prospects of each firm with respect to financial performance over the next three years. Which firm or firms would you recommend to an investor?

Assignment

1. 🌐 Prepare a set of presentation materials summarizing the information described in the paragraph above and be prepared to make a presentation using those materials.

2. 🌐 Write a report summarizing the information described above and including your conclusions about the prospects of each firm.

⊕ CASE 2: Alternative Web Page Targets and Styles

The appropriate look and feel of a web page is very much affected by its purpose and target audience. Web pages can be developed for a variety of purposes including: marketing or direct sales of a company's products, provision of on-line technical support for customers, providing effective on-line access to information sources - such as, a library or documents of a government agency, providing a variety of personnel or other job related information to employees through an internet, or providing a meeting place for computer users sharing common interest - such as, a hobby or sport. The computer skills of users and the degree of formality of the environment in which the web pages will be used will also substantially affect the structure and style of a web page.

Identify three successful web sites that differ substantially in their purpose and style. Identify and describe the principal purpose of each site. Find examples illustrating differences in the style and approach of each site and assess how well these differences fit the varying purposes and target audiences of the three web sites.

Assignment

1. ⊕ Prepare a set of presentation materials summarizing your results and highlighting key findings. Include sample screen captures from the sites or links that can be used to call up the appropriate pages in an oral presentation. Be prepared to present your results.

2. ⊕ Prepare a report summarizing your results and including web site addresses to key pages illustrating your main points.

⊕ CASE 3: Work Group Computer Upgrade

Your work group is about to purchase a set of equipment to upgrade its computing capabilities. A committee was formed to evaluate needs, and this group has come back with a set of recommendations. They have recommended the purchase of two types of PCs, one for power users and one for all other employees. There are sixteen employees in your work group. The committee is tentatively planning to order 6 high end PCs for power users and 10 less powerful "Standard PCs" for the other employees. However, at least 10 employees have requested the power PCs, so the committee would like to be able to look at the cost of increasing the number of power PCs that are purchased.

The specifications for the two types of PCs are as indicated below. Both types of units should include a 3.5 inch floppy disk and a CD-RW (read/write) device. (Note, these specifications reflect typical PC configurations at the time this casebook was written. Adjustments to several of the hardware specifications may be needed as configurations continue to evolve.)

	Power PCs	Standard PCs
Microprocessor Speed	3.0 Gigahertz	2.6 Gigahertz
RAM	1,024 Megabytes	512 Megabytes
Hard Drive Capacity	120 Gigabytes	40 Gigabytes
Monitor	19 Inch flat Panel	17 Inch

You have been asked to go out to the Internet and obtain pricing information for your work group's proposed purchase. You are asked to get at least three price quotes for each type of equipment that is to be purchased. You are also asked to investigate the warranty and servicing provided by each potential supplier. You are to gather this information, into a spreadsheet file and a set of presentation materials that can be presented to the screening committee at its next meeting.

Assignment

1. ⊕ Based on the description provided, go out to the Internet and get price quotes for all of the hardware described in this case from at least three vendors. You may need to look for a separate set of vendors for the printers. Once you have obtained the needed information, design and build a spreadsheet application that will allow you to show the costs of purchasing this hardware from each vendor. Also be sure that your application allows you to change a parameter value to see the effect of changing the number of power PC units that are purchased. (NOTE: If you are uncertain about how to design this application, read Chapter 3 for additional tips on designing spreadsheet applications)

2. Prepare a set of presentation materials that you would use to present your results to the next committee meeting. Be sure to include a discussion of the warranty and servicing provided by the alternative vendors and a recommendation with appropriate justification.

🌐 CASE 4: Strategic Use of the Internet and E-Commerce

The Internet and, more specifically the World Wide Web, is being exploited by many businesses to gain strategic advantage. Firms have used their Internet presence to pursue a variety of corporate strategies including - low cost production and product differentiation strategies, as well as, product innovation strategies. In the product innovation arena some firms have succeeded in redefining an industry or establishing an entirely new form of product.

Assignment

1. 🌐 Select a company that is recognized as having a successful E-Commerce based strategy. Write a report on your company including the following elements. Using the Internet, as well as, traditional library sources as needed, document your company's history in the use of E-Commerce. Describe and give illustrations (based on their web site) of the strategy your company is following. Describe the competitive market in which your company is operating. What new strategic actions are on the horizon in this industry? Based on your research, assess the prospects of your company over the next three years and make your best estimate as to the strategy your company will be pursuing three years from now.

2. 🌐 Prepare a set of presentation materials summarizing the findings of your report. Be sure to include links to key pages of your company's web site that illustrate its current strategy.

🌏 CASE 5: Assessing the Effectiveness of Web Pages

Examine the web sites of at least three organizations in detail. These organizations need not be in the same industry or type of business, but should have enough similarity in what they are trying to accomplish with their web sites to allow a reasonable comparison to be made. You are to rate the web sites of these organizations on a rating scale and also to reproduce screens from the web sites that you found particularly well designed, or poorly designed.

To perform your ratings create a weighted list of criteria where the weights add up to 100. You might use the content, organization, navigation, economy, and security (CONES) criteria that were described in Chapter 1 as a starting point. Add any other criteria that you feel are important.

Next you will assign a set of importance weights to your list. The set of weights you choose should add up to 100. More weight should be placed on criteria that you feel are more important. There is no right or wrong way to assign weights, but you should be able to justify the weights you choose. Once your criteria list is determined, evaluate each site with respect to each of your criteria. Use a scale of 1 to 5 for each of your criteria, where a 5 means the site did an excellent job on that criteria and a 1 means the site was very poor with respect to the specified criteria.

When your ratings have been completed place them in a spreadsheet file. In this file you will multiply the score for each of the criteria by the importance weight to develop an overall score for each site. Compare the performance of your site and determine which site had the highest total score.

Assignment

1. 🌏 Perform the assessment described above. In addition to creating the evaluation spreadsheet, prepare a paper contrasting key elements of the sites you examined and discussing the basic design elements exemplified in these sites. Be sure to include examples of well and poorly designed elements to help illustrate your points.

🌐 CASE 6: Assessing Alternative Types of Web Sites

Organizations use web sites for a wide variety of purposes. Common types of web sites include:

- Sites offering an electronic library of documents or information retrieval services (Online reference services, many government web sites, Dun and Bradstreet)
- Sites providing a range of information for individuals with a particular hobby or interest (Sites of national and regional clubs and associations)
- Sites offering customer service information (Sub-sites of computer hardware and software vendors)
- Sites supporting online job applications (Sub-sites of most large corporations)
- Sites providing products or services for online purchase (Online bookstores)
- Sites providing product information and contacts for non-online purchases (Universities, auto manufacturers).
- Sites offering online auctions or reverse auctions (e-Bay)
- Sites linking a customer to all providers of a desired product or service (Expedia, Travelocity)

as well as, many others. It is obvious that the web is being used to support widely varied goals and strategies. Investigate at least two web sites in each of three widely varied types of sites (6 sites in all).

Assignment

1. 🌐 Based on this information write a report describing the purpose of each type of site you investigated, discussing how the organization of the web sites is affected by their purpose, and comparing the web sites you investigated in each category. Assess the effectiveness of the sites you examined and suggest improvements or extensions that you would like to see.

2. 🌐 Prepare a set of presentation materials summarizing the findings of your report. Be sure to include links to key pages of your company's web site that illustrate its current strategy

🌐 CASE 7: Creating a Personal Web Site

Create a personal web site utilizing at least three linked web page (HTML) files. The initial screen on your home page should include references to the locations of at least three sub-topic areas within that web page. Sub-topics should include, at least, education, career and job information, and hobbies or personal interests.

Create a separate web page file that is organized as a professional resume and which can be referenced from the career section of your personal home page. On the resume web-page include links to example reports, applications, and web page that you have developed in this or other classes which would provide prospective employers with examples of your best work.

Create at least one additional web page that is linked to one of the other sub0topics of your home page.

Create any additional topics of interest to you and make your web site as complex as you like. Remember to apply the basic design concepts described in Chapter 1 as you develop your site.

🌐 CASE 8: The Appleton Appliances Web Site

Create a basic site suitable for use by Appleton Appliances. This web site should cover at least the following topics:

A.   store hours and location (including a map to which a user can link),

B.   a table of price information for the appliances Appleton's sells (see data below),

C.   pictures and descriptions of each of the appliance models sold by Appleton Appliances,

D.   biographical information about the sales staff, and

E.   a link to the service department web page that was used as an example in Chapter 1 and is available on your data disk.

Create mock descriptions of the appliance models and biographies of the sales staff. Use simulated pictures and maps as appropriate. Use the models and prices shown below for the price table.

	Manufacturer	Model	Price
Refrigerators	G.W.	IC280	$689.95
	G. W.	IC560	$925.95
	Kool-Air	RF380	$609.95
	Kool-Air	RF 390	$749.95
Stoves	G.W	HT280	$619.95
	G.W	HT450	$829.95
	Cooking-Aid	EL582	$499.95
	Cooking-Aid	EL584	$649.99
	Kool-Air	ST250	$479.95

Assignment

1. 🌐 Using the design principles described in Chapter 1 create a web site for Appleton Appliances using the information above and filling in with simulated data as needed. Be sure to link to the service department file that is on your data disk. In addition, add at least one more supplementary web page file exploring some element of Appleton's business in additional detail.

2. 🌐 Create a simulated web site for a small business or other web application of interest to you. Be sure to apply the design concepts covered in Chapter 1 to the web site design you create.

⊕ CASE 9: An Industry Analysis Web Site

NOTE: If you have completed Case 1 of this chapter, skip the next two paragraphs and use materials from the paper you prepared for that case to create the web site described in the assignment.

Select at least three firms in an industry of interest to you (or an industry assigned by your instructor). Using the web, research important trends in this industry and investigate each of your firms. Use standard web search techniques to find out about trends affecting the industry, then search for specific information about your selected firms. In addition, go to the web sites of your selected firms and examine their press releases and their recent annual reports for information about their current performance and strategy. Include quantitative data summarizing trends in stock prices and earnings per share.

Based upon this research summarize the most important factors expected to impact the industry over the next three years, briefly describe the current market position of each of your firms, describe the strategy being followed by each firm, and assess the prospects of each firm with respect to financial performance over the next three years. Which firm or firms would you recommend to an investor?

Assignment

1. ⊕ Using the design principles described in Chapter 1 create a web site presenting your industry analysis research results. The structure of your home web page should include at least: 1. an introduction, 2. a section on industry trends and prospects, 3. links to separate pages assessing each of your individual companies, and 4. a summary analysis comparing the your selected companies with respect to their current market conditions and prospects for the future. The pages you create for the individual companies should describe at least their current market position and strategy. Your site should include links to the home pages of the companies you studied and links to other on line sources you used in your analysis.

2.   🌐 If you completed Case 7, add a link to this report to the resume section of the personal web page you created for that case.

CHAPTER 3: DEVELOPING SPREADSHEET APPLICATIONS

End user applications can vary greatly in scope and complexity. Some applications simply require the development of a single spreadsheet for one time use by a single user. At the other extreme, end users now often develop application systems involving multiple users accessing sensitive data that must be maintained for repeated use. Clearly, the need for an extensive set of design procedures is more critical for the latter type of application.

In this chapter, we will describe some design tools and methods that are useful even for very simple spreadsheet applications. We will be assuming that the applications we are designing have only one direct user, do not have extensive data storage and control requirements, and are applications which can appropriately be developed using a spreadsheet package. Other design tools and methods appropriate for use with more complex types of applications will be discussed later in this casebook.

The development process for simple end user applications can be viewed as having three components:

1. Analysis and Design
2. Coding
3. Testing and Documentation.

In the sections below, we will present a sample case of a problem that can be addressed by a simple spreadsheet application and then describe how such an application might be developed.

THE WESTERN WATER COMPANY CASE

The Western Water Company has used a two-tier price structure for its industrial customers. This price structure was originally designed to encourage water usage. Industrial customers have paid 9 cents a gallon for the first 100,000 gallons used each month, and 7 cents per gallon for each gallon beyond the first 100,000.

Because of a water shortage in the area, and increasing consumer pressure, Western is planning to change its rate structure to one that encourages conservation. The plan is to retain the two-tier pricing structure, but reverse the tiers so that a higher rate is paid for gallons used beyond some cutoff level. For example, the rates might simply be reversed so that customers would be charged 7 cents a gallon for the first 100,000 gallons and 9 cents a gallon for all additional gallons. Another possible rate structure might be 6 cents a gallon for the first 50,000 gallons and 9.5 cents for all additional gallons. The new rate structure should produce approximately the same revenue as the previous structure. It is important for Western to know how the new rate structure affects individual industrial customers, since opposition can be expected from any customers whose water costs are substantially increased. Western has asked us to create a spreadsheet model that will allow the analysis of the impact of alternative rates and cutoff levels.

Although the price changes are designed to reduce water use, Western does not have a good estimate of how much reduction will occur. Therefore, for the purpose of this spreadsheet analysis, we will assume that the number of gallons used by each customer is unaffected by the changes in the rate structure.

ANALYSIS AND DESIGN

Analysis of a potential end user application addresses the fundamental components of an information system: input, processing, output, storage, and control. Figure 3-1 provides a pictorial representation of these system components and the questions they address. In analyzing a potential application, attention focuses first on the *output* to be produced by the application. What information is needed and in what form should it be presented? Next, we must look at the *input* data to be supplied to the application. What data are available? from what sources? and in what form? Then we must examine the *processing* requirements. What operations or transformation processes will be required to convert the available inputs into the desired output? Among software packages available to the developer, which package can best perform the operations required? We may find that the desired output cannot be produced from the inputs that are available. If this is the case we must either make adjustments to the output we expect to produce or find additional sources of input data. The fundamental elements of input, processing, and output are present in all applications.

Figure 3-1

Components of an Information System

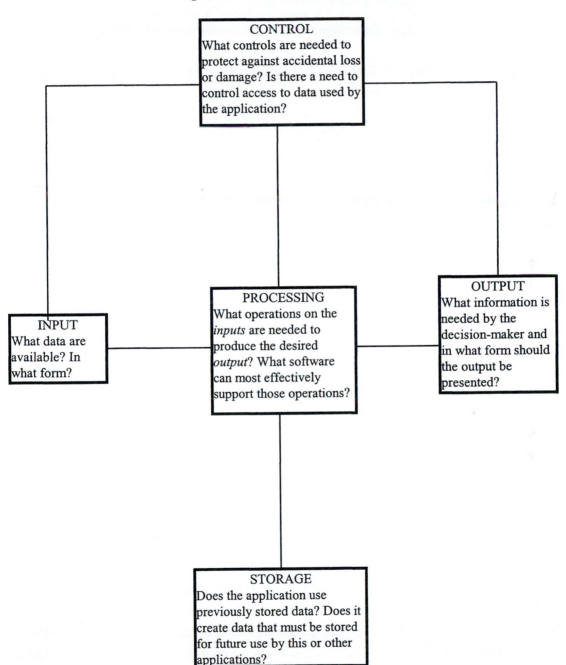

CONTROL
What controls are needed to protect against accidental loss or damage? Is there a need to control access to data used by the application?

INPUT
What data are available? In what form?

PROCESSING
What operations on the *inputs* are needed to produce the desired *output*? What software can most effectively support those operations?

OUTPUT
What information is needed by the decision-maker and in what form should the output be presented?

STORAGE
Does the application use previously stored data? Does it create data that must be stored for future use by this or other applications?

Most spreadsheet applications are interactive. This means that the user enters values in certain areas of the screen (input) and sees results on the same screen (output). The term *graphical user interface* or GUI is commonly used to describe this interface for this type of interactive application. This perspective combines input and output design to provide a unified perspective of managing the user's interactions with the application.

Spreadsheet software is best suited for applications of an ad-hoc nature that do not require systematic storage of data for future use. While spreadsheet applications have been used to store and maintain critical data this practice is undesirable. Applications requiring extensive amounts of data or the creation of data that must be stored for future use are better suited to database development. Thus, in this chapter we will assume that our applications do not require a distinct, formal, storage element. We will describe the storage element in conjunction with our discussion of development methods for database applications in Chapter 5.

Necessary control measures for applications vary greatly depending upon the: scope and duration of the application, the number and nature of the users of the application, and the nature of the data involved. For the application presented here and the cases presented in Chapter 4, we will be assuming that no special procedures to restrict access to data are needed. We will also assume that each application will be utilized either by one individual serving as a developer/user or by a developer and a single additional user. Control measures will be needed to protect against accidental loss or damage to an application file. The most basic protection against this type of loss is simply to *make backup copies of application files on a frequent and systematic basis*. If a spreadsheet application is to be used on a repeated basis or used by an individual other than its developer, it is important to *use the cell protection features of spreadsheet software to protect key cells from accidental erasure*.

When PCs are connected to a network, a decision must be made about where to locate an application. An end user developed application that is designed to serve a large number of users over a long period of time may need to be placed on a network file server. If this is to be done, there should be a common set of standards with respect to quality and control that must be met before applications are placed on the server. In this book, we assume that all of the applications are limited enough in scope and in number of users affected that they should be maintained on the PCs of the users involved.

LAYOUT FORMS - A BASIC DESIGN TOOL

The output requirements of applications are often depicted visually through layout forms. A layout form is simply a mock-up of what a report or screen should look like. It shows titles and headings for rows and columns along with either sample data or descriptions of the data that are to be presented in the report. In the case of spreadsheets, input, output, and processing activities are intermingled in a single spreadsheet file. A layout form can be used to record the input, processing, and output requirements of a spreadsheet application like that required by Western Water Company as is illustrated in Figure 3-2. The portions of the layout form enclosed in boxes or referenced by arrows contain samples or descriptions of what is to appear on the actual report and italicized type is used for these elements. Non-boxed areas contain literal labels and parameter values (shown in bold type) as they are to appear on the report.

Define Title and Heading Labels

We begin by selecting an appropriate title and then creating heading labels for the columns of data that need to be reported for each customer (the column headings under estimated billings in Figure 3-2). To meet the requirements of this problem, we must identify the name of each industrial customer and record their average water use. We must also have columns showing water billings under both the current and new pricing for each customer. An additional column showing the change in the water bill for each customer can help us to quickly see which customers are benefited and which are hurt by the new pricing. A total row is needed to indicate how alternative proposed rates affect the amount billed to all industrial customers.

Identify and Describe Input Data Areas

After defining the appropriate row and column headings, we must determine where the data values for those rows and columns are to come from. The name of each industrial customer along with the customer's average monthly water use is to be obtained from existing records and entered onto the spreadsheet as input data. Thus, we simply indicate an example of the data that will appear in each of these columns and describe its source. In the example, layout form descriptions of the source of data are enclosed in parentheses.

Figure 3-2

A Sample Layout Form for the Western Water Company Application

IMPACT OF PROPOSED RATE CHANGES ON INDUSTRIAL CUSTOMERS

BILLING PARAMETERS:	Existing Rates	Proposed Rates	
Base Rate:	$.09	$.99	*Parameter values to be entered*
Gallon Cutoff for Tiered Rate:	100,000	999,999	*repeatedly by users to*
Tiered Rate:	$.07	$.99	*evaluate proposed rates*

ESTIMATED BILLINGS:

Customer Name	Average Monthly Water Use	Avg. Monthly Amount Billed Existing Rates	Proposed Rates	Change in Amount Billed
Baxter Mining 182,755		$999,999.99 $999,999.99		$999,999.99
X(20) 9,999,999		$999,999.99 $999,999.99		$999,999.99
(input data from paper records of last year's customers and use)		*(computation:* *IF Water Use < Cutoff, Billing = Use x Base Rate;* *ELSE Billing = Base Rate x Cutoff Volume +* *Tiered Rate x (Water Use - Cutoff Volume)*		*(computed values:* Proposed - Existing Amount Billed)
TOTAL:	9,999,999	$999,999.99 (computed: sum of col. above		

NOTE: Once the spreadsheet has been developed and tested, all cells except those containing the proposed rate parameters should be protected, and a backup copy of the spreadsheet should be maintained at all times.

Examples of data can be shown via literal values e.g. Baxter Mining 182,755. Alternatively, generic examples of the format of columns of data may be used. Where generic format descriptions are used, X represents any alpha character and 9 represents any numeric digit. Thus the X(20) under Customer Name suggests that the actual names will be up to 20 characters in length and will contain label (nonnumeric) values. Values for the next two columns must be computed based upon the Average Monthly Water Use for each customer and the price charged per gallon. The rate structure parameters must appear on the layout form before the process for determining value in the billing columns can be defined.

Identify and Describe Parameter Storing Cells

Information about the current and proposed pricing structure is a key element of the spreadsheet. Parameter values for the new pricing structure are to be adjusted repeatedly to evaluate their effects on billings and the parameters that are entered here apply to each individual customer. These parameter values should appear in a prominent place on the layout form. In Figure 3-2 we have defined a section of the report called billing parameters. We have three parameters in each rate structure: a base rate, a cutoff volume of gallons at which a tiered rate is to be applied, and the tiered rate to be applied to gallons of use beyond the cutoff volume. We must compute billings for both the existing rates and proposed rates. Literal values are shown under the existing rates column since these are historic and unchanging values. Dummy values are used to show the type of data to be recorded under the proposed rates, and the note to the right of the column describes how the data values are to be obtained.

Identify and Describe Areas Whose Values are to be Computed

With the billing parameters placed on the layout form, we return to the columns showing the amount billed for each customer under existing and proposed rates. A generic data type description is shown and then the calculation used to determine the data values for these columns is described. Here conditional (or if) logic is required. If a customer's gallons of water use is below the cutoff volume, the customer's bill is simply equal to their water use times the base rate per gallon. However, if their use exceeds the cutoff volume they are charged at the base rate for all gallons up to the cutoff volume and are charged at the tiered rate for the gallons beyond the cutoff volume. The final column in the Estimated Billings section is the Change in Amount Billed. As the description for this column on the layout form indicates, values for this column are calculated by simply subtracting the billing for a customer under the existing rates from the billing for that customer under the proposed rate. Finally, we must describe how the data values in the total row will be determined. As the description indicates, the column of individual customer data above, is simply summed to compute the total value for each column.

Notice that we were able to describe input, processing, and output requirements of this application in our layout form. The layout form indicates which portions of the spreadsheet will contain input data and where that data will come from. It also indicates portions of the spreadsheet that will display the results of processing operations and describes the processing required to produce those results. No areas of the layout form in Figure 3-2 are explicitly specified as output areas because, for this application, all of the information on the layout form is to be included in the output report. If only a portion of the contents of a layout form is to be included in a report or other output document, the layout form would indicate the boundaries of the output area. For example, if we were only interested in summary billing information, the billing information for individual customers could be moved to a different section or worksheet page within the spreadsheet. This section would not appear on the screen or be printed when the billing parameters and totals row are displayed or printed.

Add Descriptive Notes

Descriptive notes at the bottom of a layout form can be used to describe control measures that need to be imposed as the design is implemented. In our Western Water Company example, formal control measures may not be needed if the spreadsheet is to be used only by its developer. However, suppose that the president of the company has only a very limited knowledge of how to use spreadsheets, but she wants to use the application herself to see the impact of different rate structures. Now, it would become necessary to protect the application from accidental changes to formulas or fixed data values and to keep a clean backup copy of the application at all times. The note at the bottom of the layout form in Figure 3-2 describes the control measures to be implemented.

The layout form we have just described may seem overly elaborate for such a simple application. Many experienced end users might sit down at a computer to create this sort of application with no more than a mental picture of its design. However, sketching a layout form for an application can lead to substantial reductions in development time and improvements in the appearance and functionality of the finished application. Tangible design documents, such as layout forms, become crucial for larger applications and it is good practice to sketch a layout form before sitting down at the computer to create an application of any size. For each case in this book, you will either be given a layout form, or will be asked to develop one before coding the application.

CODING

Once analysis and design have been completed, it is time to create the application in computerized form by typing in or coding the sets of data and instructions required to implement the application using an appropriate software package. The applications in this chapter are to be implemented using spreadsheet software.

To test your familiarity with fundamental spreadsheet operations, you should build a spreadsheet file to implement the Western Water Company application that we have designed. You can compare your work to the EXCEL spreadsheet file called **western.xls** which is available for download on the website for this casebook at www.mhhe.com/business/mis/morgan/5ed. When starter spreadsheets are provided for cases, they are also available at the casebook website and are in the form of EXCEL files with **.xls** extensions. Most other common spreadsheet packages will read these files.

TESTING METHODS

The most basic type of testing of applications involves simply checking the accuracy of the results produced. All computations in an application should be fully tested. You should perform manual calculations on a set of test data and comparing the results to those produced by the computerized application. The test data used should include a sample of every type of combination of data values that must be handled by the application. In our example, water use levels both below and above the volume cutoff for tiered pricing need to be tested to ensure that the application calculates all billings correctly. The application should also be tested by observing the effect of changes in key parameters. For example, in the Western Water Company application, an increase in the base rate parameter should cause an increase in the amount billed for every customer, while a change in the tiered rate should affect only customers whose water use is greater than the volume cutoff level.

In addition to testing for accuracy, applications should also be tested for clarity and user friendliness. Is the application understandable? Are key results highlighted appropriately? Is the application easy for its users to operate? These questions should be addressed in testing the application. As inaccuracies or limitations are discovered, they are immediately corrected and the application is re-tested in an iterative fashion until the user or users of the application are satisfied with its performance.

DOCUMENTATION

When an application is completed and turned over to users, it is particularly important that the users be provided with a complete and understandable set of instructions or *documentation* which will allow them to operate the application. Documentation can be in the form of separate written procedures describing the workings of an application. However, it is often appropriate to create spreadsheet applications that are self-documenting. To do this, a documentation section of the spreadsheet is created which simply contains a long label entry or a set of label entries describing how the spreadsheet is to be used. Normally, this section is placed on the first worksheet of the spreadsheet so that it will automatically appear on the screen when the spreadsheet is retrieved.

Figure 3-3 shows a documentation section that might be used with our Western Water Company example. The only independent information required by the user would be instructions on how to access Lotus and retrieve the application file. Once the application spreadsheet is accessed, the instructions shown should be sufficient to allow a novice spreadsheet user who is not familiar with the application to use it effectively.

This sort of documentation is necessary for any application that will be used by someone other than its builder. It is also crucial for any applications that will be used repeatedly over a long period of time. Even the developer is likely to forget some of the details of an application when he or she begins to use it again after a lapse of several weeks or months. Thus, each spreadsheet should have a documentation section that describes the purpose of the application, indicates who developed it and when, describes key assumptions used, and describes the steps needed to operate the application successfully.

Figure 3-3

A Sample Documentation Section for the Western Water Company Case

A

1 IMPACT OF PROPOSED RATE CHANGES ON INDUSTRIAL CUSTOMERS

2 Developed by: Ann Adams   Date Developed: Nov. 12, 1998

3 This spreadsheet provides an analysis of the effect of changes in water rate structures on billings to industrial customers.

4 To begin using this spreadsheet, simply click on the worksheet tab labeled WESTERN at the lower left of your screen.

5 You may enter trial values for the Proposed Rate Parameters in the column and their impact on billings will be automatically computed. Do not attempt to make entries in any cells except those for the Proposed Rate Parameters.

6 To get a printed listing of the results, simply click on the print icon. This will cause a report to be printed. After the report is printed, you will be returned to entry mode. You can print reports for as many sets of rates as you want by simply repeating this process.

7 When you are finished using this spreadsheet, simply Close it without saving your changes. This will retain the spreadsheet in its original form for your next session.

DESIGNING SPREADSHEETS WITH MULTIPLE SECTIONS

Spreadsheets frequently contain multiple sections. This is true even in our simple example case. With the documentation section shown in Figure 3-3, the spreadsheet has two largely independent sections. The documentation information needs to appear on the screen when the user first accesses the spreadsheet, but once it has been read the user moves on to the working portion of the spreadsheet.

Windows-based spreadsheet packages allow you to have multiple worksheet pages in a single spreadsheet file. Major independent sections of an application should be placed on separate worksheet pages. This is necessary because placing differently structured sets of information in overlapping rows or columns of a single worksheet page can cause problems. Suppose two different sections of the application occupy common rows on the same worksheet page. Now, if we need to add a row to the middle of one of the sections, this addition creates an undesired blank row in the middle of the working section. Similar problems can occur if two sections of a spreadsheet share common columns. Adding or deleting a column in one section would have unintended effects on the other section. This problem is avoided when independent sections of a spreadsheet are placed on separate worksheet pages.

In larger applications, there may be several independent sections of the spreadsheet. For example, a spreadsheet application might have a documentation section, a section to store input data, a section for storing some intermediate computations, and sections for storing two independent sets of results for output reporting. Figure 3-4 shows how such an application should be laid out. Each section is placed on a separate worksheet page. The documentation section is placed on either the first or last worksheet page. In designing this type of application, the developer may create a separate layout form to describe the design of each of the major sections of the application.

SUMMARY

The development process for end user applications has three main components:
analysis and design, coding and testing, and documentation.

Figure 3-4

Layout for a Multi-Section Spreadsheet

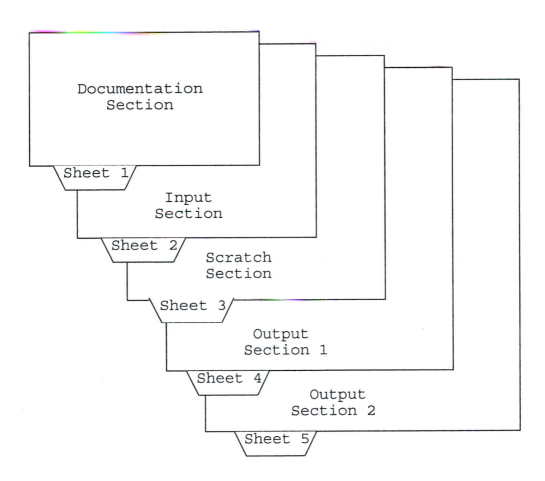

The analysis of an application focuses on the requirements of that application with respect to: the output to be produced, the inputs available, the transformation process to be used, storage needs, and the controls that should be imposed. Based upon the requirements of the application, a determination is made about the type of software to be used in developing the application. The developer then proceeds to design a solution that will meet the requirements and can be implemented using the selected software.

The layout form is a design tool that provides a visual representation of an application's design. Layout forms are most often used to document the output of applications. However, layout forms can be used to represent all components of most simple spreadsheet applications. For each spreadsheet case in this book, you will either be given a layout form for the application or will be asked to create one before you implement the application on the computer.

Coding involves the generation of computer instructions to implement the application's design using the selected software package. The spreadsheet cases presented in this casebook can be implemented using any common spreadsheet software package. Application testing involves both testing for the accuracy of processing performed by the application and testing for user friendliness. Hand calculations performed on test data are used to ensure the accuracy of an application. In addition, the user(s) of an application should test it to ensure that it is understandable to them and provides for their needs in an appropriate, user friendly, fashion. Errors or inadequacies should be corrected as they are discovered so that coding and testing occurs in an iterative fashion until all users are satisfied with the application.

Documentation provides users with the information they need to use an application effectively. Most spreadsheet applications can be almost entirely self-documenting. We can make an application self-documenting by adding a documentation section that describes the steps required to use the application effectively and documents fundamental features of the application.

CHAPTER 4: SPREADSHEET CASES

CASE 1: Kinder Care Day Care Centers

Kinder Care Day Care Centers offers pre school (day care) services and a kindergarten program. Kinder Care currently operates five centers, all of which are located in the district of Thornton. Betty Barnes founded Kinder Care five years ago in a single location in one of Thornton's upper middle class neighborhoods. This initial center was quite successful. Betty soon found that she had reached the capacity of the building she was renting and was turning away applicants. It was time to expand her operations.

Betty knew that many parents were bringing their children from distant neighborhoods to her center. She had also received numerous requests from parent asking if she could recommend a day care center in their neighborhood with a philosophy like that of Kinder Care. She began to look for additional sites in residential neighborhoods throughout Thornton. Over the last five years her operations have expanded to the current level of four centers.

As Kinder Care has grown, Betty has kept operational decision-making as decentralized as possible. She continues to serve as the director of the original center and thus has little time available to manage operations at the other centers. Her philosophy has been to hire a creative and responsible director for each center and then give that director full responsibility for, and control over, operations within their center.

A budget is established for each center based on negotiations with its director. The rates charged to customers are designed to recover a target return based on the budgeted expenses. While this freedom has attracted creative directors and a loyal customer base, Betty has found that some of her directors have had poor budget discipline or simply have paid little attention to budgetary matters. There have been several occasions, in recent years, when a director has substantially overspent their budget. To prevent similar problems in the future, Betty feels that she needs to have a better means of keeping track of performance against budget.

Record keeping at Kinder Care is currently done in manual form. Betty Barnes has used a local CPA firm to process her records for reporting and tax purposes, since the inception of her business. The reports they have produced have been effective for tax purposes and in securing financing. Betty does receive monthly reports showing expenditures by category in each center. However, these reports do not give Betty a way to quickly see when one of her centers may be in danger of significantly overspending its budget. What she would like to have is a set of summary information for each of her centers on a monthly basis showing expenses to date in each broad budget category and comparing those expenditures to budgeted levels in a meaningful way.

Knowing that you have experience in the use of spreadsheet packages, Betty asks you to try to develop a spreadsheet report that will give her the information she needs. She is able to give you a copy of the budget for each center and a set of year-to-date expenditure reports for the month just ended.

Betty indicates that expenditures in most of the budget categories tend to occur at a constant pace throughout the budget year, although some directors tend to buy most of their supplies on a once or twice a year basis. However, Betty feels that she can deal with these variations on a judgmental basis. She suggests that comparisons be based upon percentage of budget expended versus the percentage of the budget year that has passed.

She also indicates that, if your report provides the information she needs, she would like you to produce it in updated form as each month's expenses become available. She would also plan to continue running the application in succeeding years with updated budget data. As a starting point for your analysis she gives you a set of budget data for the 2004-2005 fiscal year and a set of year-to-date expenditures data for the most recent available month. This information is presented below and is available in a spreadsheet file named **Case41_kc** on the web site for this casebook.

Application Development Notes

A proposed structure for the spreadsheet and layout forms for the report portions of this application are presented in figures below. Where the layout form indicates *copy from the cell address* it means that the cell address containing this value should be used as a formula for the cell. This causes the value to be copied to the new cell and at the same time ensures that changes to the value stored in the input cell will automatically be reflected when the value is used in other parts of the spreadsheet. The proportion of the budget year that has expired serves as a parameter for this spreadsheet. The Pro-Rated Budget amounts shown are based on the assumption that expenditures should be evenly distributed over the budget year. Thus, if four months of the budget year have expired, 4/12 or one-third of the budget should have been expended.

Assignment

1. Based upon the application description and the sample design materials provided, develop a spreadsheet for the Kinder Care Day Care Centers that will help Betty Barnes evaluate each center's compliance with its budget. Your spreadsheet should have a reporting area providing the comparisons described above and should be designed to allow new year-to-date expenditures data to be quickly and effectively entered each month without risk of damaging the reporting area of the spreadsheet. Test your application for accuracy and completeness. Add a documentation section to make your spreadsheet as self-documenting as possible.

2. Using a word processing package, write a memorandum to Betty Barnes describing the procedures that you suggest she use in having your application updated each month. Incorporate copies of the output reports produced by your spreadsheet in this memorandum and add your assessment of what they indicate about the spending patterns of her arts centers.

3. Using presentation software, prepare a set of slides suitable for presentation to Betty Barnes. Your presentation should highlight areas needing attention based upon the data she provided you.

Application Cases in MIS

KINDER CARE DAY CARE CENTERS BUDGET - FISCAL YEAR 2004/2005

Expenditure Category	Dale Street	Lake Side	Trail View	Hill Ave.	West Street
Wages and Salaries	$196,500	$162,825	$212,650	$245,500	$283,725
Employee Benefits	$35,246	$29,609	$40,396	$47,643	$53,281
Supplies	$14,625	$11,600	$15,575	$22,350	$26,900
Equipment	$7,800	$8,250	$5,825	$13,275	$8,750
Utilities	$8,450	$7,825	$8,825	$11,200	$10,200
Rent	$32,000	$25,500	$26,000	$37,800	$35,000
Insurance	$10,745	$9,300	$12,650	$14,600	$14,200
Contract Services	$7,750	$8,500	$9,000	$11,550	$9,500

KINDER CARE DAY CARE CENTERS YEAR-TO-DATE EXPENDITURES
July 1 - October 30, 2004

Expenditure Category	Dale Street	Lake Side	Trail View	Hill Ave.	West Street
Wages and Salaries	$64,875	$59,347	$70,812	$93,425	$94,550
Employee Benefits	$11,725	$10,270	$13,478	$16,250	$17,755
Supplies	$5,620	$5,525	$5,015	$8,875	$7,823
Equipment	$1,857	$2,930	$2,246	$6,930	$3,841
Utilities	$1,960	$2,239	$2,632	$3,240	$3,150
Rent	$10,667	$8,850	$8,667	$12,600	$11,500
Insurance	$3,500	$3,600	$4,250	$5,175	$4,750
Contract Services	$1,855	$3,795	$3,000	$5,235	$2,900

Spreadsheet Components Diagram

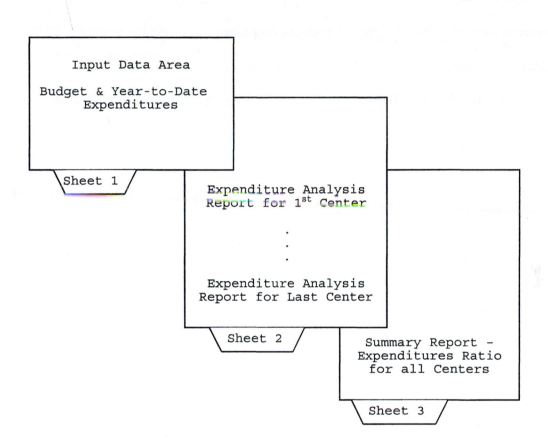

LAYOUT FORMS

INPUT DATA SHEET (Sheet 1)

As Shown in Sample data and given in the provided data file.

EXPENDITURE ANALYSIS REPORTS AREA (Sheet 2)

YEAR-TO-DATE (YTD) SPENDING VERSUS PRO-RATED BUDGET BY CENTER

REPORT PARAMETERS:

Months of Budget Year
Expired: 99 *- Input value*

% of Budget Year
Expired: 999.9% *= Months Expired / 12*

Dale Street Center

Expenditure Category	Year-to-Date Expenditures	Pro-Rated Budget Allocation	Expenditures Minus Budget Allocation	Ratio of Expenditures to Budget Alloc.
Wages and Salaries Employee Benefits *(copy from expenditure category column of input data area)*	$999,999 *(copy from cell address of corresponding cell in expend. input area)*	$999,999 *(corresponding cell from budget input data area * % of year expired)*	$999,999 *(Year-to-Date Expenditures Minus Pro-Rated Budget for item)*	9.99 *(Year-to-Date Expenditures Divided by Pro-Rated Budget for item)*
TOTAL	*(sum of column above)*			

Lake Side Center

As above and repeat for other 3 centers as well.

Layout Forms (Continued)

SUMMARY EXPENDITURES RATIO REPORT (Sheet 3)

Ratio of Year-to-Date Expenditures to Pro-Rated Budget
(Report period, e.g., July-Oct. 2004)

Expenditure Category	Dale Street	Lake Side	Trail View	Hill Ave.	West Street
Wages and Salaries	9.99	9.99	9.99	9.99	9.99
Employee Benefits					
(copy from expenditure category column of input data area)	*(copy from cell address of corresponding cell for this ratio from the expenditure analysis reports area)*				
TOTAL	9.99	9.99	9.99	9.99	9.99

🌐 CASE 2: A-1 Sporting Goods

You have been hired as general manager of A-1 Sporting Goods. A-1 Sporting Goods was founded by Ralph Jones over 25 years ago. Ralph Jones has served as general manager of the business. He is now approaching retirement age and he begun to cut back his involvement in A-1's day to day operations three years ago by assigning additional managerial duties to long time staff members.

Recently Ralph has become more and more concerned about how well his business is being managed. He fears that some of the workers given managerial responsibilities have not had good management skills. He feels that he no longer has the time required to provide oversight and leadership to the company's operations. He has hired you to provide that oversight and leadership.

A-1 Sporting Goods started with a single location and has expended to two stores: one at the original downtown (A-1 Main Street) location and one in Westridge mall (A-1 Westridge). There is a separate manager for each location. Orders are coordinated centrally to take advantage of quantity discounts, but costs are allocated back to each location and financial statements are maintained separately for each store.

Ralph Jones has provided you with annual financial statements for A-1 Sporting Goods for the past five years. You have suggested that you would like to analyze these financial statements and observe operations for a couple of weeks. Then you would like to meet with him and the managers to begin to address any problems you see. To give yourself a better feel for the status of operations, you decide to build a spreadsheet to evaluate the income statements for the past five years. You want your spreadsheet to highlight changes in revenue and cost components over time. You are preparing this application primarily for your own use. However, you plan to show printed results from this application to Ralph Jones and the managers if they show important areas of concern that require their attention.

To facilitate comparisons across years you plan to produce a set of "common size" income statements. Common size income statements express various expense and revenue categories as percentages of total sales revenue. This facilitates comparisons of the distribution of revenue and expenses over time and across business units of differing sizes.

Because you are working with data that shows trends over time, you will want to create graphs summarizing the tabular results produced by your spreadsheet. Graphical results will help you to see trends more clearly and will probably be more meaningful to Ralph Jones and his managers. You plan to create two sets of graphs: one showing overall revenue and profitability trends in dollar terms, and another showing trends in the percentage distribution of expenses.

As of now, this is expected to be a one time application. However, you are considering revising this application at some later date so that it can be updated and routinely run on an annual basis. You plan to produce printed reports and graphs from your spreadsheet for use by others, but you will be the only person serving as a direct user of the application.

The relevant income statement data for the Main Street location of A-1 Sporting Goods is shown below. To ensure that you understand these statements please note following facts about the information presented:

a.   The Other Op. Expenses category is a general category for operating expenses not covered elsewhere. It includes items such as: miscellaneous supplies and repair expenses.

b.   The value of TOTAL OP. EXPENSES is equal to the sum of all of the expense categories above it.

c.   The value of PRETAX INCOME is equal to SALES REVENUES minus TOTAL Op. Expenses.

d.   Income Tax is calculated based on PRETAX income and the applicable tax rate which may vary from year to year.

e.   The value of NET INCOME is equal to PRETAX INCOME minus Income Taxes.

A-1 MAIN STREET

	Year				
	2000	2001	2002	2003	2004
Sales Revenues	1066516	1141964	1237982	1278946	1317890
Operating expenses					
Cost of Goods Sold	432470	460872	526706	530706	536358
Wages	330126	369042	431188	438576	460016
Employee Benefits	68716	75910	85694	98014	118124
Rent	60000	60000	62400	62400	62400
Depreciation	24510	23640	21960	30500	29380
Other Op. Expenses	43216	43196	49682	40398	46706
TOTAL OP. EXPENSES	959038	1032660	1177630	1200594	1252984
PRETAX INCOME	107478	109304	60352	78352	64906
Income Taxes	37617.3	38256.4	21123.2	27423.2	22717.1
NET INCOME	69860.7	71047.6	39228.8	50928.8	42188.9

Application Development Notes

A sample layout form for this application is shown below. Two spreadsheet areas and a set of spreadsheet graphs are needed. The input data area has already been described. Data for the other location is identical in structure to that shown above and is available to you in a spreadsheet file called **Case42_A1** that can be downloaded from the web site for this casebook.

The second area of the spreadsheet is the common size reporting area that you are to create. As indicated, common size percentages are to be shown for each of the operating expense categories for each year. The common size value for an expense category is simply expenses in that category divided by sales revenue for the corresponding year.

Multiple graphs are to be produced for this spreadsheet, so you should place graphs or sets of related graphs on separate worksheet pages as appropriate. Layouts for graphs to be produced are also shown below. Data ranges to be graphed are varied, but always represent measures of one or more variable(s) over time. Thus, the set of years is the X-axis variable for each of the graphs. The graph layouts shown represent only one of many acceptable ways of displaying the requested information.

Assignment

1. Using the sample data and layout forms provided, develop a spreadsheet application which will provide analysis of trends in the financial statements of each A-1 Sporting Goods store over the past five years. Your spreadsheet should provide both reports and graphs as described in the layout forms. Be sure to test your application for completeness and accuracy. Add a documentation section to make your application self-documenting.

2. Prepare a set of presentation materials summarizing your findings. Incorporate reports and graphs as needed to highlight your main findings. These materials should be appropriate for an oral presentation to Ralph Jones and the store managers. Write a brief memorandum to Ralph Jones summarizing your key findings and describing any problem areas you found.

3. 🌐 Use the Internet to obtain data similar to that described in this case for three companies in an industry of interest to you (or an industry assigned by your instructor). *Most large corporations have an investor relations section on their corporate web site containing this type of information. You may need to combine or reorganize some expense categories to produce parallel sets of data for your companies.* Develop reports and graphs similar to those described in the layout forms above based on the data you retrieved.

4. Prepare a set of presentation materials suitable for oral presentation comparing the performance of your companies and including your assessment of their relative performance.

LAYOUT FORMS

INPUT DATA WORKSHEET

As shown above and as defined in spreadsheet file **Case41_myer**.

COMMON SIZE REPORTING WORKSHEET

A-1 SHOES COMMON SIZE INCOME STATEMENT DATA FOR YEARS 2000-2004

	YEAR	2000	2001	2002	2003	2004
A-1 MAIN STREET						
OPERATING EXPENSES		99.9%	99.9%	99.9%	99.9%	99.9%
Cost of Goods Sold						
Wages			*(expenses for this category this year /*			
Employee Benefits			*sales revenues for the corresponding year*			
Rent						
Depreciation						
Other Operating Expenses						
TOTAL OPERATING EXPENSES						

A-1 WESTRIDGE

(identical structure to the cells shown above for A-1 Main Street)

GRAPH LAYOUTS

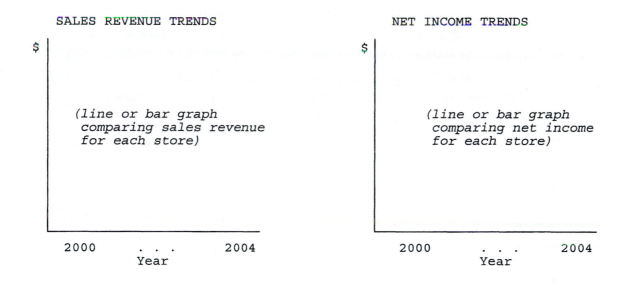

SALES REVENUE TRENDS

$

(line or bar graph
comparing sales revenue
for each store)

2000 . . . 2004
Year

NET INCOME TRENDS

$

(line or bar graph
comparing net income
for each store)

2000 . . . 2004
Year

OPERATING EXPENSE TRENDS A-1 *Xxxxxxx*

% of Sales

(bar or stacked bar graph of common
size expenditures for each of the
operating expenses categories.
Use a separate graph for each location.)

2000   2001   2002   2003   2004

CASE 3: Heavenly Herbal Tea

Charlton's Coffee and Tea Company has produced coffees and teas distributed primarily through supermarkets throughout the eastern United States for 45 years. Charlton's has a sales staff of 36 salespersons assigned to one of four regional sales managers. The regional managers in turn report to Sandra Charlton the Vice President for Marketing. The sales staff at Charlton's has always been assigned on a purely geographic basis with each salesperson selling all product lines to customers within her or his territory.

Five years ago Charlton's introduced a new product line, called Heavenly Herbal Teas (H2T). These teas contain herbs designed to stimulate memory. This new product line has proven to be quite successful, with sales reaching 18% of total company sales. However, Sandra believes that sales growth in this new product line has been hampered by the structure of Charlton's sales staff.

Sales in the new product line have been strongest among drug and health food stores and not traditional supermarkets. Some members of the sales staff have been quick to recognize the need to seek out this new type of customer, while others have not. Sandra feels that the set of customers for the H2T product line is sufficiently different to require a separate sales staff. She proposes to establish an initial sales force of four salespersons, one for each of Charlton's sales regions. Each salesperson would then be responsible for selling the H2T line throughout his or her entire region.

Sandra feels that the current sales territories need to be restructured and that some territories can be consolidated. Sandra has received approval from the CEO to make this move providing that she does not increase the total sales staff, that the salespersons for the new team are selected entirely from the existing sales staff, and that no salesperson is transferred to a different region.

Salespersons who are considered "good" candidates for the new sales team will be invited to apply. Sandra has asked you to prepare a spreadsheet for her that will identify these "good" candidates. She feels that two characteristics are particularly important. First, the H2T sales staff will have to seek out many new customers and thus the salespersons selected should have a history of seeking out new customers. Second, and most importantly, H2T salespersons should be individuals who have been enthusiastic about selling this new line. Thus, the salespersons selected should have a strong track record in sales of H2Ts. Sandra also feels that the sales quota should be considered when evaluating the performance of the sales staff. Quotas are maintained for each sales territory, and they are felt to be good measures of the sales potentials of different territories. She asks you to consider sales for the last two reporting years in your analysis.

Sandra also adds that she would like you to include a table or chart that will help her to see how much variability there is across the sales staff of each region in these two target elements. She says she wants something that will "let me know it there is enough variation in sales to new customers and sales of H2Ts to justify using them as criteria to find the sales people I need."

The information systems department was able to extract summary data from organizational databases and place it in spreadsheet format for you. This data is available on the web site for this casebook. The first 9 rows of this spreadsheet are reproduced below. For each salesperson three rows of data have been extracted, one for each year. In addition to the YEAR, the following items have been retrieved. S_NAME - the salesperson's name, REGION - the region to which the salesperson is assigned, QUOTA - the sales quota, NCUST –sales to new customers, and H2TS - sales of the H2T product line.

Application Development Notes

A sample layout form for this application is shown below. Two work sections, or worksheet pages, and a graph area are needed for this spreadsheet file. The input data should look like the sample data shown and this portion of the spreadsheet has been created for you. The second section of the application is a worksheet for the sales performance report that you are to create. The data used for this report is to come from the sum of sales from 2002 through 2004. Thus, the values for cells displaying the dollar sales amounts must be found by adding up the cells containing the 2002, 2003 and 2004 amounts. There are multiple criteria to be used in evaluating sales performance. Thus both the rate of Sales to New Customers and the Rate of Sales of H2Ts are presented. A last column called High Sales is added which is designed to identify salespersons that have shown strong performance on both criteria. Salespersons whose percentage sales in both of the target categories are more than 30 percent above average are to be identified as having high sales. Finally, in order to highlight top candidates, the data area for salespersons in each region is sorted from high to low based on Sales of H2Ts as a percentage of Sales Quota, since this is considered the most important target variable. The graph is based on the data in the Sales performance reporting area and shows both sales to new customers and sales of H2Ts as a percentage of each salesperson's sales quota.

Assignment

1. Using the input data and layout forms provided, develop a spreadsheet application to provide Sandra Charlton with information highlighting those salespersons who are good candidates to join the new sales team. Be sure to test your application for accuracy and completeness. Add a documentation section to your spreadsheet to make it as self-documenting as possible.

2. Write a memorandum to Sandra Smith describing the results of your application. Incorporate a copy of your Sales Performance Report in your memorandum. Make preliminary recommendations to Ms. Charlton based upon this report. Also suggest to her any limitations you see in the analysis and any other factors that you would suggest she look at.

3. Prepare a set of business presentation materials for an oral presentation to Ms. Charlton of the information described in 2 above.

Layout Forms

INPUT DATA WORKSHEET

As shown on the next page and as defined in spreadsheet file **Case43_h2t**.

SALES PERFORMANCE REPORTING AREA

H2T SALES PERFORMANCE BY SALESPERSON AND REGION

Region	Sales-person Name	TOTAL $ AMOUNT OF:			% of Total Sales Quota		
		Total Sales Quota	Sales to New Customers	Sales of H2Ts	Sales to New Customers	Sales of H2Ts	High Sales*
Xxxxxxxxxxx							
	Xxxx, X	$999,999	$999,999	$999,999	99.99%	99.99%	Xxx
	Xxxx, X	$999,999	$999,999	$999,999	99.99%	99.99%	Xxx
	(copy from cells in input area)	(sum of 02, 03 and 04 values for each variable from the input area)			(new customer sales / sales quota)	H2T sales / sales quota	

Average	(Average of column above)

(Data for the next region laid out as above)

(Data for the next region laid out as above)

(Data for the next region laid out as above)

* A salesperson has "High Sales" if both their sales rate to new customers and their sales of H2TS are more than 30 percent above average for their region.

(Cell value = "Yes" if sales of H2Ts >= 1.3 * Average Sales of H2Ts in the region and sales to New Customers >= 1.3 * Average Sales to New Customers in the region. Otherwise cell value is " ")

NOTE: The Sales Performance Reporting data for each region should be sorted in descending order on Sales of H2Ts as a percentage of Sales Quota

EXAMPLE GRAPH LAYOUT

```
              Distribution of H2T and New Customer
              Sales Performance vs. Sales Quota
                     Xxxxxxxx  Region
```

```
Percent of   |
   Quota     |
             |
             |
             |        (bar or line graph of Sales of
             |        H2Ts and Sales to New
             |        Customers as a percentage of
             |        Sales quota for each salesperson)
             |
             |
             |
             |_____

              Choate, D    Bates, J   Files, A   …
```

SALESPERSON

NOTE: One graph is to be produced for each Region.

Sample of Input Sales Data

S_NAME	Region	02Quota	02Ncust	02H2Ts	03Quota	03Ncust	03H2Ts	04Quota	04Ncust	04H2Ts
Bird, Lee	MA	606740	150027	101015	631615	158647	129413	675145	161280	169240
Choate, Dan	MA	798905	137925	87016	759123	117977	101236	739021	115316	124114
Evans, Mindy	MA	683675	159664	94291	722802	156539	118661	812688	161449	166123
Files, Allan	MA	810175	114410	49543	827098	120892	60379	900376	115451	80997
Jones, Alice	MA	804195	118672	55573	778988	105406	65954	773319	104526	74100
Knowles, Ken	MA	737495	194489	127727	730327	187450	147867	702549	178872	188252
Parker, Chase	MA	820640	150098	75396	794182	140985	99745	846013	137338	127041
Rowe, Cindy	MA	784415	191195	116995	771282	185541	141100	862245	191132	187470
Styles, Jack	MA	813395	165488	88296	793033	151014	111188	839056	154407	148766

CASE 4: Francesa's Southwestern Cuisine

Francesa Lewis has worked in the restaurants for over 20 years and has most recently been manager of a local restaurant in Williamsville, a town of about 30,000 in the Midwest. Francesa has decided to resign her position and go into business for herself. She plans to open a restaurant specializing in new southwestern cuisine. Currently, there are two Mexican restaurants in Williamsville, but neither of them offer the new southwestern cuisine that Francesa plans to offer.

Francesa set out to develop the information needed to project revenues, expenses, and net income for her restaurant for the first five years of operation. Based on her long experience in the business, Francesa has been able to develop rather precise estimates of her operating expenses. She has also developed estimates of expected revenues, although she feels that her revenue estimates are much more judgmental and subject to error. The information that Francesa has been able to collect about her expected costs and revenues is summarized below.

Since her operations will involve a variety of different items selling at different prices, Francesa has estimated the variable costs of operation as percentages of sales revenue. Francesa's estimates of these costs are as follows:

Food Supplies:	25%
Nonfood Supplies	6%
Labor Costs:	20%
Miscellaneous Expenses:	3%

As variable cost elements change over time, Francesa expects to make pricing adjustments that will keep the costs relatively stable in percentage terms. Thus, she estimates that the variable cost percentages shown will remain constant over the five-year period.

In addition, Francesa will face costs for the building and equipment for her restaurant and for utilities. Francesa views these as fixed costs. She does not plan to purchase either the building or the equipment. She will lease a site and rent the needed equipment based on annual lease and rental agreements. She has identified three potential sites for her restaurant. One is on Market Street downtown, the second is on Lakeview Drive at the Western edge of town, and the third is on Highway 87 at the North end of town.. The Market Street site is the most expensive, but it is also the most central location, which is likely to attract more business. The Highway 87 site, while at the north edge of town, is still readily accessible and quite visible. The Lakeview drive site has a substantially lower rent, but also is also much farther from natural traffic patterns.

Francesa plans to advertise extensively during the first year of operation in order to establish her restaurant in the minds of consumers. Because of its less prominent location, Francesa believes that she would need to spend $21,00 in advertising to establish her business at the Lakeview location, while she would need only $12,000 in first year advertising at either of the other locations. After the first year she expects to do only minimal advertising of $5,000 per year regardless of the site slected.

Francesa anticipates that the same amount of equipment will be needed at any location. Utilities costs are estimated to be $6,500 at the Main Street Location and $7,200 at the Riverview Drive location for the first year. She can sign a five-year lease for either site so that the lease cost will remain constant over the five year period. However, most of her equipment is rented on an annual (or shorter) basis Francesa expects equipment rental costs to increase about 3% per year and she expects utilities costs to increase by 2% per year. These rates of increase will be the same in either location. Her estimates of the annual costs for the building, equipment, and utilities are as follows:

```
Site Lease:
     Market Street site:     $98,000
     Lakeview Drive site:    $66,000
     Highway 87 site:        $87,000

Advertising First Year:
     Market Street site:     $12,000
     Lakeview Drive site:    $21,000
     Highway 87 site:        $12,000
Advertising - Year 2 thru 5:  $5,000 (per year)

Equipment Rental:             $24,000 (+ 3% per year increase)

Utilities:
     Market Street Site:     $12,500    (+ 2 % per year
     Lakeview Drive Site:    $14,200     increase)
     Highway 87 Site:        $14,800
```

Francesa also has developed estimates of projected sales levels. She expects that she should be able to have sales of $525,000 at the Market Street site by the second year of operation. Because the Lakeview Drive site is more remote, she would expect only $375,000 in sales by the second year at that site, while. She feels that the Highway 87 site is almost as good as Market Street, and could generate a sales level of $500,000 by year 2. Francesa also has some definite ideas about how the level of sales will change over time. Her experience has shown that sales for this type of business in its first year are typically only about 65% of the level achieved in the second year. After the second year, she expects sales to grow at about 10% per year for the remainder of the first five years. Her revenue estimates can be summarized as follows:

```
Base Sales Level (2nd year Sales):
    Main Street site:              $525,000
    Riverview Drive site:          $375,000
    Highway 87 site:               $500,000
First year sales percentage:       65%
    (% of base sales level)
Growth rate for 3rd and
    succeeding Years               10%
```

Francesa would like you to create a spreadsheet based on the estimates above. She wants this spreadsheet to provide projections of sales revenues, costs by category, and net pretax income for each of the first five years. She also wants these projections to be presented for each of the three potential sites for comparative purposes. Because many of the estimates she has given you are subject to uncertainty or error, she would like to be able to interact with the finished spreadsheet herself to see the impact of changes in any of the estimates she has made. Net pretax income is equal to sales revenue minus total cost. Total cost is equal to total fixed cost plus total variable cost. All of the other formulas to be used in generating the needed projections have been described above.

Application Development Notes

A proposed set of layout forms for this application is presented below. The spreadsheet will have a parameters section and a projections reporting section. Since there is very little input data for this case, no data file is provided. All of the estimates provided in the discussion above are really parameters that are used to generate the projected values in the reporting section. To allow maximum flexibility for what-if analysis, each parameter must be fully described in the parameters section and its value must be entered just one time in the appropriate cell of the parameters section. All uses of a parameter in the calculations of the reporting section should reference the cell address where the parameter is stored. In fact, all formulas in the projections reporting area should only contain computations based on cell references - references to cells in the parameters area and/or references to other cells in the projections area. No formulas should contain numeric literal values. It is very important to test your spreadsheet by changing each of the parameter values and checking to ensure that appropriate changes occur in the projections area. Once your spreadsheet has been completed and tested, the areas containing formulas should be protected from accidental damage. Only the cells containing parameter values should be left unprotected for Francesa's use.

Assignment

1.   Based upon the application description and sample design materials provided, develop a spreadsheet for Francesa's Southwestern Cuisine restaurant that will help Francesa Lewis evaluate the revenue prospects of each potential site. Your spreadsheet should have parameter and reporting areas as described above, and should allow Francesa to change selected parameters and see their impact on the projections. Test your application for accuracy and completeness. Add appropriate controls to allow Francesa to use the spreadsheet with minimal risk of loss or damage. Add a documentation section to make your spreadsheet as self-documenting as possible.

2.   Write a memorandum to Francesa Lewis and attach a disk containing a copy of the spreadsheet file you created for her. Also include a printed copy of the set of projections for the base parameters she supplied and projections generated by at least two other sets of parameter values. Your memorandum should highlight key findings and should include a detailed description of procedures Francesa will need to follow to use this application.

3.   Prepare a set of presentation materials appropriate for an oral presentation of your results to Francesa.

Layout Forms

PARAMETERS AREA (Numeric values shown are literal parameter values)

COST AND REVENUE PARAMETERS FOR FRANCESA'S RESTAURANT

	All Sites	Market Street Site	Lakeview Drive Site	Highway 87 Site
SALES REVENUE:				
Base Sales Level (Year 2)		$525,000	$375,000	$500,000
1st Year Sales as a % of Year 2	60.0%			
Ann. Sales Growth Rate Years 3-5	15.0%			
VARIABLE COSTS (as % of Sales Revenue):				
Food Supplies:	25.0%			
Nonfood Supplies	6.0%			
Labor Costs	20.0%			
Miscellaneous:	3.0%			
FIXED COSTS:				
Building Lease (each Year)		$98,000	$72,000	$87,000
Equipment Rental (Year 1)	$24,000			
Utilities (Year 1)		$12,500	$14,200	$14,800
Advertising (Year 1)		$12,000	$21,000	$12,000
Advertising (Years 2 through 5)	$5,000			
Annual % Increase in:				
Equipment Rental Cost:	3.0%			
Utilities Cost:	2.0%			

INCOME PROJECTIONS AREA

FRANCESA'S RESTAURANT 5 YEAR INOCME PROJECTION

YEAR

MARKET STR. SITE:	1	2	3	4	5
Sales Revenue:	(1st Yr. Sales % * Base Sales Level)	Base Sales Level	(1 + Sales Growth Rate * Prior Year's value)		
Variable Costs:					
Food Supplies					
Nonfood Supplies	(Percentage parameter for this cost element * Sales Revenue for this year)				
Labor					
Miscellaneous					
TOTAL	(Sum of above 4 items)				
Fixed Costs:					
Building	(Lease parameter value)				
Equipment	Equip. Rental parameter value	. ((1 + Equipment Rental cost growth parameter) * Prior Year's value)			
Utilities	Utilities parameter value	((1 + Utilities cost growth parameter) * Prior Year's value)			
Advertising	Year 1 Advertising Parameter value	Year 2 Advertising Parameter Value			
TOTAL	(Sum of above 3 items)				
TOTAL COST:	(Sum of Variable and Fixed cost Totals)				
NET INCOME (Pretax):	(Sales Revenue minus Total Cost)				

LAKEVIEW SITE

(Projections for this site parallel the structure for the Market Street site above.
The Base sales level, Year 1 Advertising, Lease Cost, and Utilities cost are based on unique parameter values.)

HIGHWAY 87 SITE:

(As described for Lakeview site)

NOTE: The sizes of several rows and columns in the projections area were distorted to allow room for entry of the descriptions of the formulas to be used.

🌐 CASE 5: Harrison School District

The Harrison school district has experienced budget problems for several years. Pay raises to employees have averaged less than the increase in the cost of living over the past 10 years and in 6 of the past 10 years salary levels have been frozen. Staffing levels have been cut to the point where it is felt that further reductions in staffing cannot be made without seriously reducing the level of services provided. The school district budget remains tight and there is little prospect of gaining approval of tax increases to augment the budget.

The district's budget problems have been compounded by the fact that certain categories of personnel related expenditures, most notably health insurance costs, have been increasing in an uncontrollable fashion. The district has always paid all of the costs of health insurance for its employees and their dependents. The cost of health insurance has risen sharply for each of the past five years and the district's insurance carrier is raising its rates another 12 percent for the upcoming year.

Harrison school district's business manger Tom Smith investigated several other potential insurance carriers when he received word of the rate increase. He was unable to find a better rate for comparable coverage. He next spoke with the district's current insurer about alternatives. They were able to propose a revised policy that would raise some deductibles and limit some coverage. This revised policy would cost 4 percent more than the current cost of the existing coverage (8 percent less than the cost of existing coverage for the upcoming year). However, this would represent a reduction in the level of benefits provided to district employees. The district has never reduced benefit levels in the past.

Preliminary budget meetings have been held with school superintendent Evelyn Anders to develop a proposed budget for the new fiscal year. The superintendent has reluctantly agreed that the district will fully fund the increased health insurance costs. However, given the poor revenue outlook for the coming fiscal year, she is only willing to do this if the salaries are frozen for the year. If employees are willing to accept the modified health insurance coverage package, she is willing to grant a raise equivalent to the amount of cost savings that this reduction in coverage will generate.

An employee relations committee was created four years ago. This committee has membership representing both teachers and staff and is designed to give employees a chance to be involved in budget and policy decisions. The proposed salary and benefits package for the coming year are to be presented to this committee. Tom Smith anticipates that his meeting with the employee relations committee will be a difficult one. If committee members are to be "won over" to acceptance of the budget constraints for the next year, they must become convinced of the severity of the impact of rising employee benefit costs on the district's budget. Only then will Tom be able to focus attention on the available choices.

Tom wants to be able to present summary information to the employee relations committee showing how the district's personnel costs have changed over the last five years. He has several ideas about how the data should be presented. As far as possible, he wants data to be expressed on a per employee basis. This gives committee members a better feel for the magnitudes involved. He wants the data to be organized in a way that highlights the impact of increases in employee benefit costs over time. He suggests that a five year historical period should be used. He wants the information to be conveyed graphically when possible. However, he wants the graphically presented information to be backed up by printed summary tables. Experience has taught him that some committee members are skeptical of graphical presentations and question "where the numbers came from."

Tom has asked you to prepare a set of spreadsheet reports and graphs highlighting the information he has described to you. You have been able to secure the set of data shown below from historic budget and personnel files.

PERSONNEL EXPENSES (in $1,000)

Expense Category	Year 2000	2001	2002	2003	2004
Wages and Salaries	$19,364	$19,208	$19,020	$19,470	$19,296
Health Insurance	$1,184	$1,340	$1,446	$1,844	$2,332
Retirement	$1,452	$1,440	$1,425	$1,460	$1,447
Other Benefits	$676	$674	$684	$710	$718
Employer SS Taxes	$1,898	$1,882	$1,964	$2,004	$2,020
EMPLOYMENT LEVEL	621	599	593	590	585

Application Development Notes

Since the amount of data used in this case is quite small, no input data file is created for you. You will want to create appropriate labels and enter the data shown in the tables above. You will want to create an area showing expenditures on a per employee basis, and time trends for those per employee expenditures. You should also create several appropriate graphs. Since more than one graph is needed, name and save each graph as you create it. In general, line or bar graphs are good for showing trends. Pie charts can be very effective for showing the relative size of components of something.

Assignment

1. Based on the descriptions and data above, design a layout form or set of layout forms for this application. Develop a spreadsheet to implement your design. Be sure to test your application for accuracy and completeness. Add a documentation section to your spreadsheet to make it as self-documenting as possible.

2. Write a memorandum to Tom Smith to accompany copies of the key reports and graphs produced by your application. In this memorandum, summarize major features and areas of concern that you see in the results.

3. ⊕ The chair of the employee relations committee has informed Tom Smith that the committee does not feel that they can make a decision of this magnitude without getting input from all interested district employees. She requested that the analysis you have been preparing be placed on the district's web site so that district

employees and other interested individuals could examine the figures prior to the negotiations. Tom agreed to this and has requested that you summarize your results in the form of a small set of linked web pages that will briefly describe the situation and will allow read access to the graphical and quantitative information.

CASE 6: Midwest Restaurant Supply

Midwest Restaurant Supply is a wholesaler of restaurant supplies and equipment. Midwest began as a supplier of coffee and coffee making equipment to restaurants. Over the years, Quigley's business has expanded to include a wide variety of nonperishable, expendable restaurant supplies and all types of restaurant equipment.

The sales staff at Midwest Restaurant Supply are paid primarily on a commission basis. They receive a modest base salary that is adjusted once a year and a commission whose amount is calculated monthly based on three components. A percentage commission is paid on sales of supplies, a different and higher percentage commission is paid on sales of equipment, and a bonus amount is paid for each new customer found by a salesperson. *Currently these rates are 1.5% on supplies, 2.5% on equipment and $50 per new customer.*

Commission rates are set by the Vice President of Marketing, Jan Jones. Ms. Jones likes to make adjustments to the commission rate structure occasionally to provide appropriate incentives. For instance, if equipment sales are slow and equipment inventory is up, she may temporarily raise the commission percentage for equipment. Similarly, if she feels that the sales staff has not found enough new customers lately she may raise the bonus for new customers. When adjustments to the commission structure are made, they are effective at the beginning of the next calendar month.

Because of the complexity and changing nature of the commission system used, commissions have always been hand-calculated. Midwest uses a PC based accounting software package to handle its order processing and billing. That package is used to produce a monthly summary listing of sales of supplies, and sales of equipment for each salesperson. Each salesperson submits a list of new customers they have attracted that month. This list is verified from the accounting data to determine the count of new customers.

Ms. Jones has requested that you create a spreadsheet for her that will show the amount of commission and bonus, as well as, the total gross pay owed to each salesperson. She also wants to see totals for commissions paid for sales of supplies, commissions paid for sales of equipment, and bonuses paid for attracting new customers. She asks that the spreadsheet be designed to allow her to easily make adjustments to any of the commission rates when needed. She indicates that she would like to be able to turn the spreadsheet over to her secretary to do the actual data entry each month. The secretary to Ms. Jones has experience in using word processing on the computer but is a novice spreadsheet user.

Application Development Notes

A set of input data for this application is shown below and is available in a spreadsheet file called **Case46_mrs** on your data disk. This data represents the summary sales data for the most recent month. Your spreadsheet should treat all commission and bonus rate information as parameters. That is, all uses of a given rate should reference a single cell that can be easily identified and modified by the user. Your application should contain an area displaying detailed information about commissions earned by component and salesperson, as well as, summary information for each salesperson and for the staff as whole.

Sample of Monthly Sales Data

Salesperson Name	Salary	Month	Supplies	Equipment	New Customers
Moran, Sue	$575.00	8/1/2004	$64,889.00	$56,120.00	6
Murray, Ben	$500.00	8/1/2004	$49,319.00	$57,240.00	1
Peterson, Pamela	$575.00	8/1/2004	$55,085.00	$45,344.00	5
Sanders, Arnold	$550.00	8/1/2004	$60,068.00	$71,416.00	3
Garland, John	$625.00	8/1/2004	$67,589.00	$53,344.00	6
Franklin, Jim	$475.00	8/1/2004	$64,889.00	$56,120.00	6

Assignment

1.   Based on the description above and the data provided, design a layout form for this application. Using this layout form develop a spreadsheet meeting all the requirements of this application. Make sure that your application contains appropriate control measures. Test your spreadsheet for accuracy and completeness. Add a documentation section to make your spreadsheet as self-documenting as possible.

2. Write a memorandum to Jan Jones describing this application. Include a copy of a sample set of output based on the sample data and rates provided. A copy of a disk containing your spreadsheet application should also accompany this memorandum. Make sure that you memorandum describes a set of procedures to be used by Ms. Jones and her secretary for the entry and processing of new data each month. Make sure that your memorandum, or the spreadsheet documentation section, addresses appropriate backup and control measures.

🌍 CASE 7: Craft Corral

Craft Corral is a regional chain of craft and hobby supply stores operating in the upper Midwest. The original Craft Corral store was located in Minneapolis. Initially Craft Corral expanded by opening new stores in other locations in the Minneapolis St. Paul area. Soon, Craft Corral's management adopted a strategy of expending by acquiring existing craft stores. Using this strategy Craft Corral has expanded to a total of 35 stores in 16 cities.

Ed Anderson, CEO of Craft Corral, has been very successful in finding good acquisitions for his company. He looks for non-chain hobby or craft stores with a good customer base. He finds that there are often stores of this type which have established a good reputation in their area and are well organized and operated, but which are having trouble competing with the volume buying power of chains. When an acquisition is made, it is through a friendly takeover. Ownership of the acquired store is usually given the option of purchasing Craft Corral stock and an attempt is made to retain as much of the staff of the acquired store as possible.

Ed Anderson is considering expanding to a new City. Martindale is a city with a population of about 140,000 that has experienced rapid population growth in recent years. Ed would like to establish a store in Martindale to get a foothold in this market. Three stores in Martindale have been identified as possible targets for acquisition. Financial statements for the year just completed for each of the three target stores have been obtained and are presented below.

Ed asks you to prepare a set of reports for him based on these statements. He wants to see comparisons across the target stores based on their most recent income statements and balance sheets. He also wants your report to include calculations of three key financial ratios for each target store: the current ratio, the inventory turnover rate, and a measure of return on investment. He indicates that this type of analysis is needed each time the company is considering a new acquisition.

The balance sheet and income statement categories shown below are a rather typical (though highly aggregated) set of categories for retail establishments. The financial ratios requested by Mr. Anderson may be defined as follows:

1.   The current ratio for a company is simply its total current assets divided by its total current liabilities.

2.   The inventory turnover rate is the number of times per year a store's inventory is turned over (sold). It is equal to the cost of goods sold from the income statement divided by the inventory amount in the asset portion of the balance sheet. (The inventory value used in computing this rate normally involves averaging the inventory level on the current balance sheet with that for the immediately prior year. Here we are assuming that the level of inventories has not changed significantly over the course of the year. Thus, we use the level of inventory at the end of the year as an estimate of average inventory throughout the year.)

3.   The return on investment that Mr. Anderson is interested in is the rate of return on total owners' equity. This is equal to the net income from the income statement divided by total stockholders' equity form the balance sheet.

Since the stores involved differ significantly in size, you will use common size financial statements to facilitate comparisons between them. Common size balance sheets show the values of categories of assets, liabilities and owner's equity as a percentage of total assets. Common size income statements show the values of revenue and expense categories as a percentage of sales revenue.

Application Development Notes

The set of balance sheet and income statement data shown in the table below are also available in a spreadsheet file on the web site for this book in a file called **Case47_cc**. You should create a reporting area of your spreadsheet that will display common-size financial statements and the requested financial ratios for the three stores in a side-by side fashion to facilitate comparisons.

Assignment

1.   Based on the descriptions and data provided, design a layout form for this application. Use your layout form to develop a spreadsheet that will meet the requirements for this application. Test your application for accuracy and

completeness. Add a documentation section to make your spreadsheet as self-documenting as possible. Get a printed listing of the reporting section of your spreadsheet.

2.   Suppose you were asked to convert this application into a spreadsheet template for use in comparing the financial statements of up to five different companies. Write a short paper describing key problems and limitations to providing such an application. Describe in general terms how you would modify your spreadsheet to allow it to be used as a general template, and describe the types of control and back-up measures that would be required for such an application.

3.   ⓐ From the Internet, obtain recent financial statements of three firms in an industry of interest to you, or assigned by your instructor. Create a spreadsheet that will produce the analyses described in this case for those two firms. Add graphics to highlight key comparisons. Prepare a set of presentation materials summarizing your results.

FINANCIAL STATEMENTS FOR TARGET COMPANIES

COMPANY

BALANCE SHEETS	Hobby Loft	Kraft Barn	Creative Crafting
ASSETS			
Current Assets			
Cash	$268,972	$192,988	$309,152
Accounts Receivable	$235,896	$269,564	$345,800
Inventory	$588,144	$700,932	$503,720
Other Current Assets	$44,924	$53,080	$65,120
Total Current Assets	$1,137,936	$1,216,564	$1,223,792
Long Term Assets			
Land	$0	$248,000	$296,200
Building	$0	$712,000	$970,000
Equipment	$776,640	$745,360	$730,100
Less: Accumulated Depreciation	($192,980)	($549,712)	($310,160)
Total Long Term Assets	$583,660	$1,155,648	$1,686,140
TOTAL ASSETS	$1,721,596	$2,372,212	$2,909,932

	Hobby Loft	Kraft Barn	Creative Crafting
LIABILITIES			
Current Liabilities			
Accounts Payable	$292,968	$233,280	$273,680
Taxes payable	$77,708	$95,372	$89,132
Other Current Liabilities	$33,012	$10,940	$14,356
Total Current Liabilities	$403,716	$339,592	$377,168
Long Term Liabilities			
Notes Payable	$0	$100,000	$0
Other Long Term Liabilities	$61,000	$0	$100,000
Total Long Term Liabilities	$61,000	$100,000	$100,000
TOTAL LIABILITIES	$464,716	$439,592	$477,168
Stockholders' Equity			
Paid-in Capital	$940,000	$1,380,000	$1,500,000
Retained Earnings	$353,572	$512,620	$374,348
Total Stockholders' Equity	$1,293,572	$1,892,620	$1,874,348
TOTAL LIABILITIES AND STOCKHOLDERS' EQUITY	$1,758,288	$2,332,212	$2,351,516
INCOME STATEMENT			
SALES	$708,215	$775,357	$890,532
OPERATING EXPENSES			
Cost of Goods Sold	$362,820	$373,954	$411,230
Employee Wages and Benefits	$223,627	$238,727	$295,791
Other Operating Expenses	$48,635	$75,263	$53,270
Depreciation	$12,215	$24,095	$17,240
Interest	$2,315	$8,257	$3,844
Total Operating Expenses	$649,612	$720,296	$781,375
PRETAX INCOME	$58,603	$55,061	$109,157
Income Taxes	$19,929	$18,320	$38,364
NET INCOME	$38,674	$36,741	$70,793

CASE 8: Milford Financial Services

Milford Financial Services is a financial services company headquartered in Boston Massachusetts. Milford along with many other companies in the industries has gone through substantial changes in recent years. Extensive use of computer systems and the ability of customers to directly order financial services via the web, have caused substantial changes in the way employees do their jobs. There is a feeling that morale and relationships among the employees has suffered due to the rapid pace of change. In addition, employee turnover is at an all time high.

Cindy Sanders, the Vice President of Human Relations at Milford, feels that programs encouraging employee interaction outside the work environment can help to both reduce turnover and improve employee morale. Such programs can help to strengthen social relationships between employees and help to build those relationships more quickly. The increased camaraderie created should also improve overall morale and reduce employee turnover.

One program that has come to Cindy's attention is the offering of free or reduced-rate health club memberships to employees. Such a program would be offered through a health club facility very near the Milford office complex. This would make it easy for Milford employees to use health club facilities before or after work, or even during the lunch hour. By promoting use of health club facilities around the time and place of work, it is felt that employees will schedule activities together or simply "run in to each other" in the health club facility. Another consideration in Cindy's mind is the fact that several competing financial services firms have begun offering this "perk" to their employees. Cindy feels that it is time to investigate the costs of such a program.

She begins her investigation by examining the types of health club membership options offered by related firms in the area. She discovers that some larger firms have their own "in plant" facilities. Many firms do not offer health club services at all. The remainder offer free or reduced price memberships to a health club with at least one facility within the immediate area of their offices. When memberships are offered, they cover only the employees themselves, although health clubs often offer discounted rates for covered employees who want to establish family memberships.

Cindy also engages in some informal conversations with a variety of employees. These discussions suggest that free health club memberships would be viewed as a significant benefit by many employees, particularly if the membership included the availability of free aerobics classes. Based on these preliminary discussions, Cindy decides to investigate the costs of fully supporting memberships for all employees. She begins discussions with health clubs. She is able to find three health clubs with nearby facilities that are willing to offer a corporate membership for Milford employees.

1.   Firm-it-up operates a single facility which is located two blocks from the Milford offices. It offers a full range of health club services, although Only very limited aerobics classes are offered. The owner is willing to guarantee that additional classes will be added to meet Milford's needs if Milford signs a contract with his club.

      Firm-it-up's owner quotes Cindy a flat rate of $25 per membership per month for a basic membership not including aerobics classes. He would charge $40 for a premium membership including aerobics classes. Firm-it-up would charge Milford only for those employees who signed up for memberships and would charge the premium rate only for those employees signing up for aerobics classes.

2.   The Sweat Shop operates from a single, large-scale, facility which is located approximately 4 blocks from the Milford offices. It offers a full range of services and appears to have sufficient facilities to accommodate the needs of all Milford employees without further expansion.

      The ownership of the Sweat Shop quotes you a price of $25 for each employee per month. For this fee every employee would receive a membership including access to aerobics classes. This rate is offered with the understanding that memberships will be issued to <u>all employees</u> and Milford will pay $25 per month for all employees including those not using the health club

3.   The Fitness Factory operates five health club facilities in the greater metropolitan area. The nearest facility is approximately one-quarter mile from the Milford offices. This facility currently offers only a limited number of aerobics classes, but

all other facilities and services appear to be more than adequate. The ownership of The Health Racket is willing to commit to offering additional aerobics classes as needed if Milford signs a contract with them.

The ownership of the Fitness Factory quotes you a price of $35 per membership per month. They would charge Milford only for those employees requesting membership cards from the club and would offer aerobics classes to all members.

In order to compare this alternative to the others Cindy sees that she will need to have a reasonable estimate of the proportion of employees who would plan to attend the club and become members. To assess the first plan, Cindy also needs to know how many employees will participate in aerobics classes. She has her secretary do a quick phone survey to estimate the interest level. Because she feels interest in the health club may vary by age, Cindy has her secretary randomly select about 25 employees from each of four age categories for the survey. The survey categories and results are shown below. Employees are split into age categories of Under 30 years old, 30 to 39 years old, 40 to 49 years old, and over 50 years old.

```
TELEPHONE SURVEY RESULTS
                                       Number Who Would Request
                   Number
      Age         Surveyed     Membership         Classes

  Under 30           26            23                19
  30 to 39           22            16                10
  40 to 49           27            15                 8
  Over 50            24            16                12
```

To generate estimates of the costs of the alternatives the employment levels for these demographic groups are also needed. From personnel records in a database Cindy was able to retrieve the following data about the current level of employment in each demographic group used in the survey:

```
               Number of
     Age       Employees
Under 30          262
30 to 39          307
40 to 49          214
Over 50           194
```

Cindy asks you to develop a spreadsheet for her that will produce estimates of the total monthly cost of each of the three programs based on the survey and employment data provided above. Cindy indicates to you that she feels that the prices quoted by the health clubs are negotiable. However, she feels that each club will stick with their current rate structures. For instance, Firm-it up might drop their rates to $22.50 for base memberships and $35.00 for premium memberships, but they would continue to insist on issuing a premium membership to all employees participating in aerobics classes. Similarly the Sweat Shop might cut their membership rate a dollar or two, but they would continue to insist that Milford buy a membership for every employee. Cindy wants you to create a spreadsheet that will allow her to easily enter changes in rates that she might be able to negotiate and immediately see their impact on the costs of a plan.

Application Development Notes

Because the amount of input data to be processed is small no input data file is provided. You will need to enter the survey and employment level data and use it to provide data that can be applied to the sets of rates offered by the three health clubs. To estimate the number of employees in each demographic group who will participate in the health club, calculate the percentage of participation based on the survey and multiply that by the number of employees in the given age and marital status group. Make sure that every element of the rate structure for each of the health clubs is entered as a parameter that can be modified by changing the value of a single cell.

Assignment

1. Based on the descriptions and data described above, design a layout form for this application. Based on your design, develop a spreadsheet to meet Cindy's requirements. Be sure to test your application for accuracy and completeness. Be sure to add appropriate controls that will allow Cindy to change the rate parameters associated with the three plans with minimal risk of destroying or damaging the application. Add a documentation section to your spreadsheet to make it as self-documenting as possible.

2. Write a memorandum to Cindy to accompany a disk containing your spreadsheet application. This memorandum should include any instructions needed to access and

run your spreadsheet. You should also discuss the key assumptions made and note any limitations you see in the data and analysis methods used.

CASE 9: Luminous Lighting Corporation

The Luminous Lighting Corporation is a manufacturer of light fixtures and lamps. Luminous Lighting sells its products to furniture stores and lighting specialty stores. Luminous Lighting distributes a catalog describing its products to wholesalers and retailers throughout the United States and they can place orders either through the mail or over the phone, based on the catalog information. Luminous Lighting's catalog and ordering system is also available on-line and many customers now place their orders on-line.

Luminous Lighting's sales are almost exclusively on a charge basis. That is, an order is filled and a bill for payment is shipped along with the order. Bills are due 30 days from the date of shipment. To encourage rapid payment of bills, Luminous Lighting offers a two percent discount on all orders whose billings are paid prior to the due date. Billings which are not paid within 30 days after the due date (within 60 days of the shipment date) are considered delinquent. An interest charge of two percent per month is charged on these bills. Bills not paid within 120 days of the due date are referred to a collection agency.

John Oliver is head of the Accounts Receivable Department at Luminous Lighting Corporation. He feels that it is very important that he keep abreast of trends in the levels of sales, receivables, and flows of payments. Mr. Oliver gets a monthly Receivables and Payments Report from the corporate IS department showing totals for key sales, receivables, and flow of payments variables. The summary portion of this report is shown below.

Receivables and Payments Report: Summary Section
(All dollar values in thousands)

Total Monthly Sales:	$34,415
Total Accounts Receivable:	$41,985
Receivables over 30 days delinquent:	$8,719
Receivables over 120 days delinquent:	$3108
Total Payments Received:	$32,083
Discount Qualified Payments:	$16,912
(Paid within 30 days of billing)	

The Receivables and Payments Report shows the current status of several key variables, but does not provide time trends. Mr. Oliver would like to have monthly reports and graphs displaying trends in these variables. He would also like to have the data for these variables readily available to him on his PC so that he can perform ad-hoc analysis when necessary.

The amount of data required to meet Mr. Oliver's needs is quite small, it is in aggregate form and is not considered to be sensitive or subject to restricted access. Also, the IS department at Luminous Lighting Corporation has a substantial application backlog. For all of these reasons, Mr. Oliver believes that an application to meet these needs can and should be developed within his department, rather than referring it to the IS department for development.

Mr. Oliver is an experienced user of spreadsheet software. However, his schedule does not permit him to develop this application personally. He asks you to develop it for him. He indicates that he wants the application to store 12 months of summary data from the Receivables and Payments Report. He also wants a standard report and a standard set of graphs based on this data to be produced each month.

As you discuss the particulars of the application with Mr. Oliver, you find that he wants a report that tracks a set of ratios over time. The ratios he wants to track are: the ratio of accounts receivable to monthly sales, the ratio of receivables over 30 days delinquent to total accounts receivable, the ratio or receivables over 120 days delinquent to total receivables, and the ratio of discount qualified payments to total payments received. The report should show a chronological history of these ratios for the past year.

In addition to this report, Mr. Oliver wants to have three graphs produced each month. Each graph should plot the dollar values of a set of variables over time. The first graph should plot trends in three variables: total monthly sales, total accounts receivable, and total payments received. The second graph should plot total accounts receivable, receivables over 30 days delinquent, and receivables over 120 days delinquent. The final graph should plot total payments received and discount qualified payments.

Mr. Oliver provides you with the set of summary data from the Receivables and Payments Reports for the past year shown below.

Receivables and Payments Reports Sample Data
(All values in thousands of dollars)

Period	Sales	Accounts Receivable	Receivables 30+ days Late	Receivables 120+ Days Late	Payments Received	Discount Qualified Payments
Nov, 03	$31,080	$37,119	$7,221	$2,433	$29,781	$16,083
Dec, 03	$31,251	$37,410	$7,326	$2,487	$29,850	$16,083
Jan, 04	$31,422	$37,707	$7,437	$2,541	$29,916	$16,077
Feb, 04	$31,593	$38,001	$7,545	$2,595	$29,985	$16,074
Mar, 04	$31,761	$38,298	$7,656	$2,652	$30,051	$16,071
Apr, 04	$31,932	$38,598	$7,767	$2,706	$30,111	$16,065
May, 04	$32,103	$38,895	$7,878	$2,763	$30,177	$16,056
Jun, 04	$32,274	$39,198	$7,992	$2,820	$30,240	$16,050
Jul, 04	$32,442	$39,495	$8,106	$2,877	$30,300	$16,041
Aug, 04	$33,090	$40,286	$8,285	$2,957	$30,906	$16,328
Sep, 04	$33,780	$41,110	$8,490	$3,013	$31,502	$16,603
Oct, 04	$34,415	$41,985	$8,719	$3,108	$32,083	$16,912

Application Development Notes

Because of the small amount of input data used for this application, no data file is provided. You should store the summary data shown above in an input data worksheet. This data area will be used to supply the raw data needed for the report and graphs. The summary report requested by Mr. Oliver should be produced on a separate worksheet. Additional worksheets should be used for each of the 3 graphs needed for this application.

Assignment

1. Based upon the description above and the sample data shown, generate an appropriate set of analysis and design aids for this application. Using these aids develop a spreadsheet application to fulfill all of the requirements of the case. Test your application for accuracy and completeness.
2. Prepare a set of presentation materials that you could use to demonstrate your application to Mr. Oliver and to give him full information about the procedures he needs to follow in operating and maintaining this application.

CHAPTER 5: DEVELOPING DATABASE APPLICATIONS

In this chapter, we will describe design and development tools and methods that are appropriate for simple database applications. Much of the development process described in Chapter 3 applies, not just to spreadsheet applications, but to the development of all types of applications. However, we will see that there are some unique features to database applications that require variations in the development process used. Before discussing the development process for database applications in detail, we will first discuss the relative strengths and weaknesses of spreadsheet and database software packages. This should give you a feel for making decisions about which type of software to use for a particular application.

CHARACTERISTICS OF SPREADSHEET AND DATABASE PACKAGES

When a choice of software packages is available, it is important that the developer select the package, or combination of packages, that is best suited for the application to be developed. Thus, it is appropriate at this point to briefly discuss the capabilities and limitations of spreadsheet and database management packages. Although both spreadsheet and database packages have capabilities in all of the key areas required for an application (output, input, processing, storage, and control), each has distinct strengths and weaknesses. A list of key strengths of spreadsheet and database packages is shown in Figure 5-1.

Spreadsheets have an intuitive user interface that is often easier for end users to grasp and work with than the interface offered by database packages. Spreadsheets also feature strong and flexible processing capabilities that allow one to quickly perform varied mathematical and statistical computations. They allow great flexibility in the layout and formatting of results for reporting and provide graphical output capabilities. Spreadsheets can provide users with strong what-if capabilities by allowing them to interact with and control their applications. Users can quickly make changes to parameters and immediately see the effects of those changes.

Figure 5-1

KEY FEATURES OF SPREADSHEET AND DATABASE PACKAGES

Key Spreadsheet Features

1. Provides an intuitive and user friendly interface that is easy for users to work with in building applications.

2. Allows relatively complex mathematical and statistical computations to be performed including comparisons of individual and summary values.

3. Allows extensive user interaction with applications and user control of parameters for "what if" analysis.

4. Allows very flexible formatting and layout of data for reporting.

5. Allows presentation of results in graphical form.

6. Allows the rapid entry and use of small amounts of data that do not need to be maintained for repeated long term use.

Key Database Features

1. Allows controlled entry and maintenance of data that is needed for sets of data that will be accumulated and used over time.

2. Allows data to be made available in a variety of sorted orders and selected subsets that might be required for different applications.

3. Allows summarized or selected data to be quickly and easily provided when needed for reporting purposes.

4. Allows logically related data from multiple files to be linked together.

5. Allows the same data to be used, in different forms and sorted in different ways, in a variety of different output documents.

Limitations of spreadsheets mainly revolve around their handling of data. Spreadsheets are not particularly effective in handling large amounts of data that may need to be collected over a period of time, and used later. It is also difficult to use a spreadsheet in situations where a common set of data or selected portions of a common set of data need to be used to produce many different reports.

These data handling capabilities are the main strength of database management software. Database packages are designed to accommodate the entry and maintenance of data in table structures that are separate from the report and query components of an application that are developed to produce outputs. Depending on the database software package used, these structures may be stored as separate files or they may be separate named objects within an overall database file. We will use the term object to refer to these components. The data entry environment for database packages makes it easy to enter data either in a batch mode or one record at a time as it becomes available. The data entry environment provided also has the ability to automatically detect many types of errors. In addition, forms can be created to further facilitate and enhance data entry. Since separate objects are used to perform the processing needed to produce reports or other output, it is easy for one set of data to be used for several applications producing a variety of different outputs.

Database packages also allow the linking together of logically related data that may have been stored in separate files. Many database applications require the use of multiple linked tables of data. Some of the cases presented in this casebook are designed so that they can be developed using only a single data table, but several others require the use of two or more related tables. In describing the development process for database applications, we will initially assume that a single table is used. A later section of this chapter will describe the changes required when multiple related tables are used.

Database packages also have significant processing capabilities. Processing that requires summarization of data, sorting of data, or selection of data can be accomplished quite readily by a database package, and often these applications are better suited to database packages than to spreadsheets. The querying capabilities built into database software make it particularly effective in dealing with unanticipated, ad-hoc, requests for selected information that has been gathered to satisfy the needs of other applications.

At the same time, several important types of processing can be accomplished much more simply in a spreadsheet than in a database package. Many of the complex mathematical and statistical computations that are readily handled by spreadsheet software are much more difficult to implement using a database package.

Based upon these characteristics, we can make some generalizations about the types of applications that can best be developed using database software. Applications that have strong requirements for the storage and maintenance of a set of data to support varied uses should be developed using database software. Applications that require complex computations performed on relatively small volumes of data are better suited to spreadsheet development.

Of course, some applications require capabilities that are best provided by using spreadsheet and database software together. For example, data may be stored and maintained in database files. Then selected or summarized data may be retrieved from the database and placed in a spreadsheet. The spreadsheet can then be used to provide flexible computational capabilities, the manipulation of parameters, and the ability to produce graphical output. Application software product "suites" often allow data from a database to be linked into a spreadsheet. The values of certain spreadsheet cells are defined as formulas that reference specified data from a related database table. When this type of linkage is used, changes to data in the database table will automatically appear in the related spreadsheet file the next time it is accessed.

In the remainder of this chapter, we will describe some design and development tools and methods that are appropriate for database oriented applications. We will also briefly discuss the design and development of applications requiring the integrated use of database and spreadsheet packages. To facilitate this discussion, a case suitable for development as a database application is presented below. We will describe the development process in the context of that case.

THE TEES ARE WE CASE

Tees Are We is a supplier of T-Shirts to athletic teams and other groups. Tees Are We produces its shirts to order and guarantees delivery within 3 working days. All orders placed must be for a total of at least 15 shirts. Customers may select from a number of predefined designs or may request a custom design. Four sizes (small, medium, large, and extra large) are available. Only one design is allowed for each order, but a variety of shirt sizes may be requested on a single order. For example, a customer could place an order for 5 medium, 12 large, and 3 extra large shirts of a particular pattern.

Tees Are We has always used a manual order system. The necessary information for processing an order is recorded on an order form. This information includes the customer's name and phone number, the order date, the number of units of each size ordered, and the design selected. Customers can select predefined designs from a design book. The design number of the selected design is then recorded on the customer's order form. If a custom design is desired, a drawing of the design is made and approved by the customer and this drawing is attached to his or her order.

A copy of each new order is placed at the bottom of a stack of pending orders. Orders are filled one at a time from the top of the stack. The shirt printing machine is set up to imprint the selected design for each order as it is processed in turn. This method ensures that orders are filled in the order that they were placed, but it does not necessarily lead to efficiency in production.

In particular, the store manager has noticed that there are often multiple pending orders requesting the same design. Set up time could be reduced if all of these orders could be filled with a single production run. The manager also has had difficulty in controlling his inventory of shirts of different sizes. Deliveries are sometimes delayed due to shortages of some shirt sizes, while other shirt sizes are substantially overstocked. Information about the number of units of each shirt size needed to satisfy each day's pending orders would help him do a better job of managing his shirt inventory. The manager of Tees Are We would like us to develop a computer application to address these problems.

ANALYSIS

Analysis of a potential end user application seeks to identify the requirements the application must meet with respect to each of the fundamental components of an information system. Those components were described in Chapter 3. We seek to identify the output, input, processing, storage, control, and user interface requirements of the application.

For the applications we have designed thus far, it has not been necessary to record the results of the analysis stage in written form. However, as the size and complexity of applications increase it becomes increasingly important to have written notes of the key requirements of an application. The form in which these requirements are recorded will depend upon the complexity of the application and the skills and needs of its developer and users. Figure 5-2 shows an example of an Application Requirements Report that might be used for the Tees Are We case. This report simply records, in summary narrative form, the requirements of the application with respect to each of the major information system components. It serves as a guide for use during design and implementation to ensure that all of the requirements are met. This type of information should be sufficient to document the requirements of most end-user developed applications.

For the Tees Are We case, two formal outputs need to be produced: a report listing all pending orders, sorted by design type, for use in managing production runs, and a report listing the total number of shirts of each size ordered on each day. The third item listed under output in Figure 5-2 relates to ad-hoc reporting needs and is described further below.

Input data for the application are supplied by the customer as each order is placed. The data needs to be stored in an organized fashion for later retrieval. We will have to ensure that enough information is gathered from the customer to allow the required output to be produced, and that this information is stored effectively. The transformation processes required are relatively simple. Data must be sorted in the appropriate order for each output report and individual data values must be added to produce summary totals.

Control and user interface requirements are an important consideration for this application. The data used in this application are not of a personal or sensitive nature and, thus, access controls are not required. However, this application stores and maintains important organizational data. Thus, it will be necessary to establish procedures for making back-up copies of the application's files. Also, individuals with limited computer experience will use parts of this application. Ideally, sales staff should be able to enter a

Figure 5-2

**Application Requirements Report
for the Tees Are We Case**

Output Requirements

A report of pending orders sorted and subtotaled by Design Type is to be produced.

A summary report showing the number of shirts of each size ordered on each order date is to be produced.

Support should be provided for ad-hoc retrievals of names and phone numbers of selected customers whose orders have various characteristics.

Input Requirements

All input data are to be obtained from customers during the order taking process.

Processing Requirements

Required processing includes sorting on design type and order date respectively and calculating some totals and subtotals.

Storage Requirements

Input data are to be collected as each order is placed, and stored for periodic reporting. Data for each order will be retained until that order is filled.

Control / User Interface Requirements

Sales staff are to input data for new orders only.

Corrections, report generation, and deletion or migration of filled orders are to be performed only by the manager or the assistant manager in the manager's absence.

A back-up copy of the pending_orders data file is to be made at noon and just prior to closing each day.

new order record as each order is placed. They will need a simple user interface and step-by-step instructions describing how they are to use the application. Also, we likely will want them only to perform data entry activities. Other activities, such as correcting errors in records that have been created and deleting records for orders that have been filled (or migrating them to another file), should be the responsibility of one individual who has a good working knowledge of the software used to implement the application.

Analysis of Ad-hoc Output Needs. The ability to produce ad-hoc output whose specific nature cannot be determined in advance is an important feature of database applications. For example, the manager of Tees Are We might discover that a particular design has been lost or damaged, or that he is out of one size of shirt and will not be able to get a shipment for several days. In either event, he would like to be able to quickly retrieve a listing of pending orders affected by the problem, so that he can contact the affected customers.

Database applications should be designed to provide maximum support for this kind of ad-hoc reporting. The actual production of ad-hoc reports is accomplished using the query capabilities of database packages to retrieve selected data from a stored database as the need arises. Although we cannot predetermine which specific design type or shirt size the manager will want to inquire about, we can anticipate the *type* of information that will be needed. We can ensure that the application that is developed stores and maintains the types of data that users are likely to need on an ad-hoc basis. For example, in the Tees Are We case, neither of the pre-specified output reports necessarily requires that the customer's phone number be input and stored in the database. However, in our analysis of the application, we would anticipate the types of ad-hoc output needs that are likely to arise and provide the kinds of data required to fulfill those needs. Thus, we would be sure to include the customer's phone number in the input data to be collected and stored. The final entry under *output* in Figure 5-2 describes this requirement.

Software Selection. Normally, the decision about the type of software package to be used to develop an application is made immediately after the analysis of the application's requirements has been completed. This application is clearly one that can best be developed using database software. It uses data that needs to be placed in computerized form as each order is received and that data must be maintained for periodic reporting. It involves multiple output reports, which are derived from the same set of data. In addition, users are likely to need to retrieve selected portions of the stored data for ad-hoc reporting. Finally, it has only very simple processing requirements, which can easily be handled by database software.

DESIGN

The design of an application provides a visual representation of the elements needed to meet an application's requirements. The design should provide a pattern for the actual implementation of the application. For spreadsheet applications, a single spreadsheet file implemented all application components. Thus, we were able to represent the entire design of the application using one design tool, the layout form.

Database applications use a diverse set of component objects. Initially, there is a process for creating a table. Creating a table actually creates and stores a definition of how a table is organized - things like what data fields are to be stored and their data type and length. This defines the structure that is used to collect *input* records and to *store* data. Once the table structure is defined, data must still be entered into the table. Data can be entered, updated, and displayed using a standard table display, or a custom form object can be created to handle these functions.

Often it is necessary to *process* the data stored in a table and convert it into the format desired for *output* reporting. Reports objects are created to perform these functions. The distinction between forms and reports is that forms can be used for data entry or modification as well as display, while reports are used only to display data. Several different reports may be developed from a single table. Each report is created as a separate object.

The layout forms we described in Chapter 3 are a good tool for describing report and form objects. However, the layout form is not a good tool for describing the table structure specifications needed to support database input and storage requirements. Here, the key need is to define the structure of the data to be collected and stored. A design tool, which we will call the Data Dictionary Form, can be used to record this type of information.

DATA DICTIONARY FORMS

As we have already noted, database management software is normally used when there is a need to store and maintain data in an organized fashion to support the production of multiple types of output. Databases are designed to work with groups of data that can be thought of as fitting into a table structure. This table structure also corresponds to a standard file structure. That is, there are a number of instances of something (a person or thing) that we are gathering data about, and we must be gathering the same set of characteristics for each instance. In the Tees Are We case, we are gathering information about orders that are placed and we are interested in the same characteristics for each order – the Order Number, Order Date, Customer Name, Customer's Phone Number, Design Type, and the number of Units Ordered of each size of shirt. A sample of data for the Tees Are We case is shown in Figure 5-3. The characteristics that are recorded for each instance correspond to the field names in a file structure or the column names in the table display of Figure 5-3. Each instance corresponds to a record in a file structure or a row in our table display.

Database software requires that we define the column structure of a table before we begin to collect and store data in it. Information about the structure of a table is commonly known as *data dictionary* information. The amount of information in a data dictionary can vary.

Figure 5-3
Table of Sample Data for the Tees Are We Case

Order Number	Order Date	Customer's Name	Customer's Phone Number	Design Type	Units Ordered			
					Sm.	Med.	Lge.	Extra Lge.
1001	09/28/98	Barnes, Janet	774-3826	M32861	2	10	8	4
1002	09/28/98	Jones, Ed	525-1834	CUSTOM	0	17	22	14
1003	09/28/98	Adams, Al	779-8921	R38671	26	14	0	2
1004	09/28/98	Davis, Owen	523-3826	M32861	0	73	44	32
1005	09/28/98	Landes, Larry	775-2913	CUSTOM	10	7	3	0
1006	09/29/98	Morris, Sue	778-8371	P22371	0	8	16	4
1007	09/29/98	Bates, Nancy	773-6018	CUSTOM	28	0	0	0
1008	09/29/98	Thomas, Rob	526-9205	P22371	0	18	14	7
1009	09/29/98	Date, Charles	777-9014	R38671	16	11	3	0
1010	09/30/98	Evans, Jim	523-0145	M32861	4	31	11	6

Figure 5-4 shows a simple data dictionary form for a table that might have been used to store the data in the Tees Are We case. At the top of the form, the name of the table (**ORDER** in this case) is recorded. Below the table name, there is an indication of the control measures to be used when entering and maintaining the data of this table. Here we note that anyone on the sales staff is allowed to create a new order, but only the manager is to be allowed to modify or delete orders once they have been created. Following the description of controls, a set of information describing each column is presented. The information to be specified for each column includes:

1. A name for the column in a format that is acceptable for implementation using database software,

2. a definition or description of the data item,

3. an indication of the type and dimensions of the data to be stored in a column, and

4. an indication of whether or not the table should be indexed on this column of data.

The data type helps determine how data will be stored and used by the database software. The most commonly used data types are: character, numeric, and date. The *character* data type is used for alphabetic data and can be used for variables containing numeric digits, such as social security numbers, when they will never be used mathematically. The *numeric* data type is used for numeric data of all types that will be used in mathematical computations. The *date* data type is a special data type used just for dates.

The length specified for a column should be large enough to accommodate the largest or lengthiest entry we ever expect to use for that column. For numeric columns, we indicate both the length and the number of places required after the decimal point. The value **4.0,** shown as the length for the Sm_Units column, indicates that the column is four digits long with no digits after the decimal point. Columns with a date data type normally do not require a length specification because the database software provides a fixed length for them.

Figure 5-4
Data Dictionary Form for the Tees Are We Case

TABLE NAME: ORDER

REQUIRED CONTROLS FOR ACCESS AND USE:

Any member of the sales staff is allowed to add new order records. Only the manager or assistant manager is allowed to make corrections to order records, delete order records, or produce reports. A back-up copy of the database is to be made at noon and just prior to closing each day.

Column Name	Column Description	Data Type and Length	Indexed?
Ord#	Assigned order number from printed order pad, must be unique	Character 5	yes unique
Ord_Date	Date when order was placed in mm/dd/yy format	Date	yes nonunique
Cust_Name	Name of the customer placing this order	Character 20	no
Cust_Phone#	Phone number of customer	Character 8 e.g. 999-9999	no
Design_Type	Number of design selected from the design book or "Custom" if a custom design has been selected	Character 6	yes nonunique
Sm_Units	Number of size small shirts ordered	Numeric 4.0	no
Med_Units	Number of size medium shirts ordered	Numeric 4.0	no
Lg_Units	Number of size large shirts ordered	Numeric 4.0	no
XLg_Units	Number of size extra-large shirts ordered	Numeric 4.0	no

The last item recorded for each column is an indication of whether or not an index is needed for the column and, if there is an index, whether or not it should be unique. An index allows us to quickly retrieve data from the table sorted based on the value of the column. However, maintaining indexes consumes storage space and processing time. Thus, an index should be maintained on a column only if it is used as an identifier for rows (records) in the table, or if we will frequently need to sort the data in order based on that column. The column (or columns) used for identification is called the *primary key* and a unique index should always be created for the primary key column. In the Tees Are We case, a unique Ord# is assigned to each order and this Ord# is used to identify a particular order record. In the Tees Are We Case, we also need to produce one report that is sorted on DESIGN_TYPE and another that is sorted on Ord_Date. Thus, we will also want to create indexes on each of these columns. However, these indexes are not unique. That is, different orders are allowed to have the same Design_Type or Ord_Date. These indexes are used to identify sets of orders with a characteristic in common. At the same time, the unique index on Ord# assures that no two orders will be assigned the same Ord#.

Entity Relationship Diagrams

Entity Relationship (ER) diagrams are the most widely used design tool for presenting the structure of a database. These diagrams are designed to capture the relationships between different tables in a multi-table database, as well as providing summary information about the structure of each table (entity). Currently, our application consists of only a single table. We will discuss the relationship portion of the ER diagram in a later section. Figure 5.5 shows a sample entity diagram using ER notation. An entity (or table) is represented by a rectangular box. At the top of the box the name of the table is listed in capital letters. Beneath the table name, the names of each of the attributes of the table are listed. In our notation, we have followed the attribute names with a brief indicator of the data type and length of each attribute. In addition, if there is an attribute that can be used to uniquely identify each row of the table, a primary key attribute, that attribute is shown with an underline – the Ord# attribute in Figure 5.5.

Entity diagrams provide a concise means of initially capturing key elements of the structure of a table. However, it is still important that more detailed information, such as descriptions of the meaning of table columns, be captured if we are building a database application that will have multiple users. Most database management systems allow this type of information to be recorded at the time a table is actually created. For example, in Microsoft Access, the design view of a table provides a place to store and view descriptions of each attribute along with a great deal of other descriptive information.

In building complex organizational databases, design software is used that captures summary information about entities and their relationships in a visual ER diagram. The diagram is then linked to more detailed information, like that presented in our data dictionary form, for each of the entities. Typically users can double click on an entity in the ER diagram to pop up a display of the more detailed dictionary information. For end user applications of the scale presented here, a simple paper and pencil drawing like that presented in Figure 5-5 may be adequate to support the initial design of the database. Once they are implemented, most database systems become self-documenting with respect to their table structures. For instance, in Access, the design view of each table provides a detailed view of the contents of each table and the relationship diagram shows the relationships between tables.

Figure 5-5
An Entity Diagram for the Tees are We Case

```
         ORDER

Ord#                 C(5)
Ord_Date             Date
Cust_Name            C(20)
Cust_Phone#          c(8)
Design_Type          C(6)
Sm_Units             N(4)
Med_Units            N(4)
Lg_Units             N(4)
Xlg_Units            N(4)
```

LAYOUT FORMS

Layout forms for database applications provide information very similar to that described for spreadsheet applications in Chapter 3. A separate layout will be used for each form or report object to be produced by the application. A sample layout for a data entry form for this case is shown in Figure 5-6. The structure shown is a very simple one. We have simply formatted the screen to make data entry a bit easier for the user. Since most customers choose designs from a predefined list of available types, we could use a form element that lets the user select from pre defined choices for the Design type information.

Figure 5-6
Data Entry Layout Form for Tees Are We Order Data

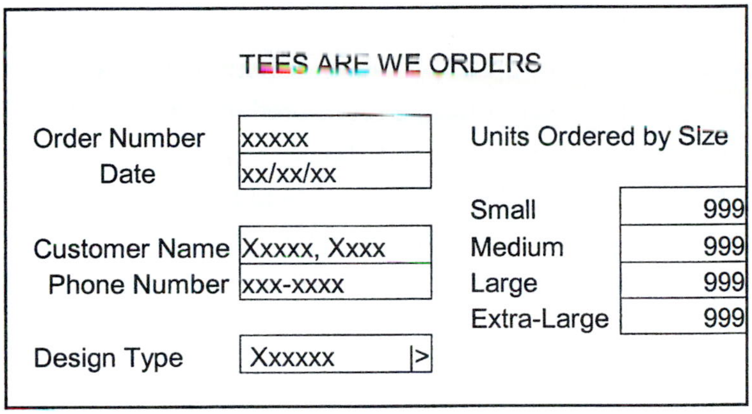

Figure 5-7
Forms Elements for Selecting from a List

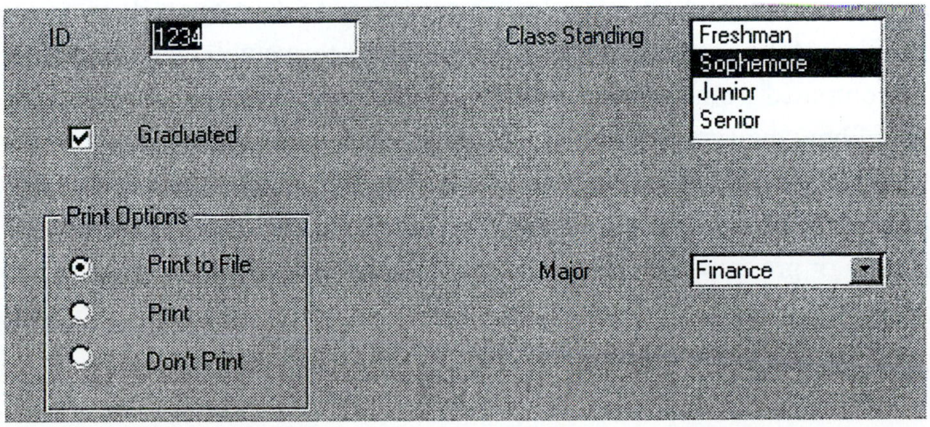

The use of lists of choices in forms elements can help reduce errors by having users pick from the valid set of choices for those elements having only a few valid choices rather than entering these values. Figure 5-7 illustrates the most common forms of limited list items. Check boxes can be used for items that have only two valid responses, such as Yes-No or True-False (Graduated in Figure 5-7). Radio Buttons are used for situations with a limited number of values – typically 3 to 5 (Print Options in Figure 5-7). Only one of the radio buttons can be selected at one time. List boxes or drop down boxes are another alternative. A list box shows all of the choices at all times with the selected item being highlighted (Class Standing in Figure 5-7). A drop down box shows only the selected item, but the user can display all available choices by clicking on the down arrow symbol next to the displayed value (Major in Figure 5-7). List boxes should not be used where there are more than 7 or 8 valid choices. Where there is a larger set of choices and whenever the user can select from a set of predefined choices or add their own value, a drop-down list or combo-box is a good choice. A drop-down list box would be an appropriate choice for the Design Type data entry field of Figure 5-6. Your instructor may ask you to use restricted list form elements in your database applications. They will be suggested where appropriate in the layout forms presented here.

Sample layout forms for the two reports in the Tees Are We case are shown in Figures 5-8 and 5-9. The data source to be used with a report is indicated above the heading in the layout form. This area describes any sort or selection operations that should be performed on the table before the report is produced. Typically, the report will be based on a query where the query performs the selection operations on the table that are described under DATA SOURCE. In Figures 5-8 and 5-9, data needs to be sorted to support grouping of the data. Boxed areas of the layout forms will contain data values retrieved or computed from the table or query. The format of these data values and descriptions of how they are to be obtained appear in the boxes (or, when necessary in brackets following the boxed area). The non-boxed information on the layout forms represents literal labels that should appear on the reports. The descriptions presented describe sorting or grouping activities and computation of subtotals and totals, since these are the processing activities for these reports.

Figure 5-8
Layout Form for the Tees Are We Case Production Scheduling Report

DATA SOURCE: ORDER Table sorted by design type.

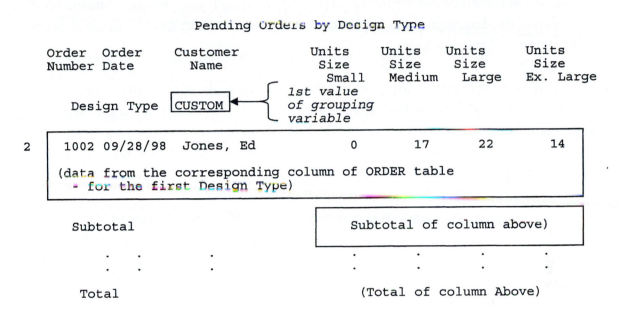

Pending Orders by Design Type

Order Number	Order Date	Customer Name	Units Size Small	Units Size Medium	Units Size Large	Units Size Ex. Large

Design Type CUSTOM ← 1st value of grouping variable

2 | 1002 09/28/98 Jones, Ed   0   17   22   14

(data from the corresponding column of ORDER table
- for the first Design Type)

Subtotal   Subtotal of column above)

.   .   .   .
.   .   .   .

Total   (Total of column Above)

Figure 5-9
Layout Form for the Tees Are We Case
Report of Daily Orders by Shirt Size

DATA SOURCE: ORDER Table sorted and grouped by Order Date.

Units of Shirts Required for Pending Orders
by Order date and Shirt Size

Order Date	Units Size Small	Units Size Medium	Units Size Large	Units Size Ex. Large	
09/28/98	28	63	122	63	Data values from query grouped by order date
09/29/98	37	55	108	72	
.	.	.	.	.	
.	.	.	.	.	
.	.	.	.	.	
TOTAL	9999	9999	9999	9999	Total of column above

CODING

When analysis and design have been completed, it is time to create your application in computerized form. This is accomplished by typing the sets of instructions and entering the data required to implement the application using an appropriate database management software package.

Details of the instructions required to implement applications will not be described here. For most database applications, you will need to follow a set of steps in sequence to code or implement your design. First, create the structure of your table following the design provided by your data dictionary form. Be sure to create any indexes needed for any sorted reports that will be required.

Next create any "forms" you wish to use when adding or modifying records in your table. As we noted above, Forms help to improve the speed, accuracy, and user friendliness of the data entry process. Where there are a limited number of possible values for a column in a table, a list of possible values can be displayed and the user selects from the list. This is easier for the user and reduces data entry errors. On the other hand, forms may not be needed for tables where data are only rarely added or modified.

Next, perform data entry operations to gather the data to be stored in your table. Once your table is populated with at least a sample of data, you can create the query and report objects required for your application.

A layout form similar to that shown for reports is an appropriate design tool for use in designing sophisticated data entry forms. However, for the cases presented here, we will assume that no layout designs are needed for data entry forms. Data are to be entered using standard editing structures of the database package or through forms whose design can be derived from the data dictionary information for the table.

To test your familiarity with fundamental database operations, you should build the table, queries, and reports required to implement the Tees Are We case. If you are using ACCESS, you can check your work against the sample file called TRW.MDB.

TESTING METHODS

The database table structures created by an application and any forms, queries, and reports produced by the application need to be tested for accuracy. Database table structures and input forms are tested by entering sample data. The data type and length defined for each field should be appropriate for the storage of all values that the field can take on. A set of sample data including extreme values for various fields should be used for testing.

Queries and reports need to be checked for the accuracy of the results they produce in the same way that spreadsheet files are tested. The computations performed by the query or report are checked by performing manual calculations for the set of test data. It is particularly important to check subtotals within reports to make sure that the data used by the report has been sorted and grouped correctly.

In addition to testing for accuracy, applications should also be tested for clarity and completeness. Do the set of outputs produced meet all of the requirements of the application? Are the headings and labels easy to understand? Do they fully describe the data presented? These questions should be addressed in testing the application. As inaccuracies or limitations are discovered, they are corrected and the application is re-tested until the user or set of users of the application are satisfied with its performance.

DOCUMENTATION

As we discussed in Chapter 1, creating documentation is an important part of the development of any application. Database applications are almost always maintained over a period of time and often are operated by multiple users. These features make documentation particularly crucial for database applications. Database table structures are automatically self-documenting to some extent, because a first-time user can look up data dictionary information on a table to identify the fields involved and the type of data stored. However, with database packages, it is not feasible to add a comment section of the type we placed in our spreadsheet files. Database applications normally require some external written documentation describing the procedures to be followed by their users. This documentation should also provide instructions for the control of the database and procedures for making periodic backup copies of your database file.

Figure 5-10 shows a set of procedures that might be used for the Tees Are We case. The procedures presented assume that the application was developed using ACCESS. Notice that a very explicit and detailed set of instructions is provided for the sales order clerks who will be using the system. The instructions describing how the manager and assistant manger are to use the application are much less detailed because we are assuming that these individuals will have a good understanding of fundamental aspects of the ACCESS software package.

Figure 5-10
Documentation of User Procedures for the Tees Are We Case

ORDER CLERKS

1. Accessing the Table. This process is to be used every morning to initially access the order table, and each time you need to access the order table after doing some other computer operation.
    a. Select the **ACCESS** icon from the opening window.
    b. Pick the **Open Database** icon
    c. Select the database name **TRW.MDB** from the list of choices
    d. Click on the **Tables** icon and the **Order** table.
    e. Select **Open** to display this table in a datasheet view permitting entry of new order records.
2. Entry of order data.
    a. You should see a blank data form for the Order table on your screen. Key in the appropriate data for each order as you process it and use the tab key to move to the next column.
    b. Before pressing the enter key after filling the last row of the form, double check all of your data and make any corrections that are needed.
    c. Press enter to save the completed record and produce a blank screen for the next order.
    d. If you mistakenly save an order record with erroneous data, have the manager or assistant manager make the needed correction.
3. Making backup copies of the database. A backup copy of the Order table is to be made at noon and just after the last order is processed each day.
    a. Open the **File Manager** window.
    b. **COPY** the **TRW.MDB** file to a file called **A:TRWBAK.MDB** on the floppy diskette labeled database backup.
    c. Use part 1 instructions to get back into the order file if more orders are to be processed.

ASSISTANT MANAGER AND MANAGER

1. You can retrieve and print two reports one called TRWDES which summarizes orders by design type and another called TRWDATE which summarizes pending orders for each shirt size on a daily basis.
2. Get a list of filled orders from production at the close of each day and migrate those orders out of the orders database file.
3. Periodically check the creation date of the backup file **A:TRWBAK.MDB** to ensure that backup procedures are being followed.

INTEGRATED APPLICATIONS

As we noted earlier, many applications can best be handled by a combination of database and spreadsheet software. Frequently, we may have an application using data that needs to be collected and stored over a period of time, but which requires analysis using complex computations or requires output displayed in graphical form. Such an application would best be handled by creating a database file to collect and store the needed data. Then, when analysis is needed, the database file could be exported to or linked to a spreadsheet. The data could then be manipulated using all of the features of spreadsheet software. In designing the layout forms for the spreadsheet application, the input area would be described as being derived from the associated database file.

In implementing this type of integrated application, the database file would be created, populated, and tested first. Then data would be exported to or linked to a spreadsheet to create a spreadsheet file containing a copy of the data extracted from the database. Finally, the spreadsheet formulas needed to produce the spreadsheet outputs would be created and tested to complete the application.

BUILDING MULTI-TABLE DATABASE APPLICATIONS

One of the most powerful features of database software packages is their ability to support applications using multiple related tables. When we described the Tees Are We case, we indicated that customers select designs from a design book. Only a DESIGN_TYPE code was recorded in our ORDER table. However, we can easily imagine that each design has a number of characteristics which could be recorded in a database table. Let us suppose, for instance, that there is a text description for each design and that there is a price for each design - some designs are more elaborate than others and thus their price is higher. Figure 5-11 illustrates this revised set of data.

Figure 5-11
Table of Sample Data for the Tees Are We Case

Order Number	Order Date	Customer's Name	Customer's Phone Number	Design Type	Design Description	Price	Units Ordered Sm.	Med.	Lge.	Extra Lge.
1001	09/28/03	Barnes, Janet	774-3826	M32861	Troubled Toad	$20	2	10	8	4
1002	09/28/03	Jones, Ed	525-1834	CUSTOM	Custom Design	$25	0	17	22	14
1003	09/28/03	Adams, Al	779-8921	R38671	Happy Face	$15	26	14	0	2
1004	09/28/03	Davis, Owen	523-3826	M32861	Troubled Toad	$20	0	73	44	32
1005	09/28/03	Barnes, Janet	774-3826	CUSTOM	Custom Design	$25	10	7	3	0
1006	09/29/03	Morris, Sue	778-8371	P22371	Einstein	$20	0	8	16	4
1007	09/29/03	Bates, Nancy	773-6018	CUSTOM	Custom Design	$25	28	0	0	0
1008	09/29/03	Adams, Al	779-8921	P22371	Einstein	$20	0	18	14	7
1009	09/29/03	Date, Charles	777-9014	R38671	Happy Face	$15	16	11	3	0
1010	09/30/03	Evans, Jim	523-0145	M32861	Troubled Toad	$20	4	31	11	6

We could simply add DESIGN_DESCRIPTION and PRICE columns to the ORDER table structure described in Figure 5-4. However, this approach would cause some problems. The DESIGN_DESCRIPTION and PRICE should be the same for all orders of a particular DESIGN_TYPE. For example Order Numbers 1001, 1004 and 1010 are all for the DESIGN_TYPE M32861. Suppose that the description of this design is "Troubled Toad" and its price is $20. We would need to type this information in for each order of the DESIGN_TYPE M32861 even though we know that the DESIGN_DESCRIPTION and PRICE should be the same for all records of this DESIGN_TYPE. This involves wasteful data entry time and increases the potential for error. A clerk might enter a DESIGN_DESCRIPTION or a PRICE incorrectly for one or more of the orders.

A more appropriate design would be one which recognizes that we have a set of information about designs that is separate from - but related to - our order information. Under this design alternative, we would create a separate DESIGN table which would have DESIGN_TYPE, DESIGN_DESCRIPTION, and PRICE as columns. The DESIGN_DESCRIPTION and PRICE for a particular design (DESIGN_TYPE) would be entered only once in this table. Figure 5-12 shows a set of sample data for this table and its structure is shown in the DESIGN entity structure of the ER diagram in Figure 5-15. Note that Design_Type serves as the primary key for this table.

Figure 5-12
Sample Data for the DESIGN Table

Design_Type	Design_Description	Price
M32861	Troubled Toad	$20
CUSTOM	Custom Design	$25
R38671	Happy Face	$15
P22371	Einstein	$20

In addition, we seem to have a set of information about customers –
CUST_NAME and CUST_PHONE#. It is very likely that we will have repeat customers -
Janet Barnes and Al Adams in the sample data of Figure 5-11, For instance. As with the
design data, there is duplication in the recording of customer names and phone numbers
and entering them repeatedly increases the chance for errors. It appears that we also have
a set of information about customers that is separate from, but related to, our order
information.

To capture our information about customers more effectively, we need to create a
separate CUSTOMER table. In this case, neither the CUST_NAME nor the
CUST_PHONE# attributes serves as a relatable identifier for a specific customer. We
might have more than one customer named Joe Smith, for instance. The CUST_PHONE#
also presents problems as an identifier; a customer's phone number is likely to change
when she or he moves and it is possible to have multiple customers with the same phone
number – roommates in a dorm, for instance. In this situation, we will assign an artificial
identifier – a CUST_ID – to each customer. We will have the database control this
number and ensure that a unique number is assigned to each customer. Figure 5-13
shows sample data for the CUSTOMER table

Figure 5-13
Sample Data for the CUSTOMER Table

CUST_ID	CUST_NAME	CUST_PHONE#
1	Barnes, Janet	774-3826
2	Jones, Ed	525-1834
3	Adams, Al	779-8921
4	Davis, Owen	523-3826
5	Morris, Sue	778-8371
6	Bates, Nancy	773-6018
7	Date, Charles	777-9014
8	Evans, Jim	523-0145

Data from multiple tables of a database can be linked together if the tables have an attribute in common and if that common attribute is an identifying attribute in one of the tables. In our example the attribute DESIGN_TYPE is included in both the ORDER and DESIGN tables. The DESIGN_TYPE is also the primary key or identifying column in the DESIGN table and it is referred to as a foreign key when it appears in the ORDER table. A foreign key attribute stands for the object it identifies and allows us to link any and all of the data describing that object with the data of the related table in which it appears. Thus, the DESIGN_TYPE column in the ORDER table allows us to identify which row of the DESIGN table is associated with each ORDER and allows us to link orders with any of the data about the related design. For example, DESIGN_DESCRIPTION and PRICE information can be shown for any order by creating a query which links rows of the ORDER and DESIGN tables having equal values for the DESIGN_TYPE attribute.

Note that the structure of the ORDER table must be modified with respect to the customer information. The ORDER table no longer contains the CUST_NAME or CUST_PHONE# columns, but instead contains the CUST_ID foreign key attribute. A sample of data for the ORDER table is shown in Figure 5-14 and the Data Dictionary Form of Figure 4 would need to be modified to include Cust_ID as an attribute and to exclude CUST_NAME and CUST_PHONE#.

Figure 5-14
Sample ORDER Table Data for Tees Are We

Ord#	Ord_Date	Cust_ID	Design_Type	Sm_Units	MED_Units	Lg_Units	XLg_Units
1001	09/28/03	1	M32861	2	10	8	4
1002	09/28/03	2	CUSTOM	0	17	22	14
1003	09/28/03	3	R38671	26	14	0	2
1004	09/28/03	4	M32861	0	73	44	32
1005	09/28/03	1	CUSTOM	10	7	3	0
1006	09/29/03	5	P22371	0	8	16	4
1007	09/29/03	6	CUSTOM	28	0	0	0
1008	09/29/03	3	P22371	0	18	14	7
1009	09/29/03	7	R38671	16	11	3	0
1010	09/30/03	8	M32861	4	31	11	6

Figure 5-15 shows an ER diagram for the revised Tees Are We Case. As we noted earlier, an ER diagram documents how the tables of a database are related, as well as describing some of the key characteristics of the columns in each table.

The Entities or Tables are represented by rectangles with the name of the table at the top and its column names listed underneath. The identifying or primary key columns are underlined and foreign key columns are shown with a dotted line under them to help us find them more readily. In our version of the ERD, we have also included a brief indicator of the data type and length of each column.

The lines connecting the tables document how they are related to each other. The end that shows multiple lines (or "crow's Feet") connecting to a table means that there may be many related items in that table. Thus, the line from CUSTOMER to ORDER indicates that several orders may be associated with one customer – multiple lines into the ORDER table, but each order must be associated with only one customer – only a single line into the CUSTOMER table. Finally, a circle on the line near one of the tables is used to indicate that it is possible that there are no related items in that table. The circle near the ORDER table on the line from the DESIGN table indicates that we may have a design with no related orders – such as, new design that we are just getting ready to introduce to customers.

Figure 5-15
An Entity Relationship Diagram for the Tees Are We Database

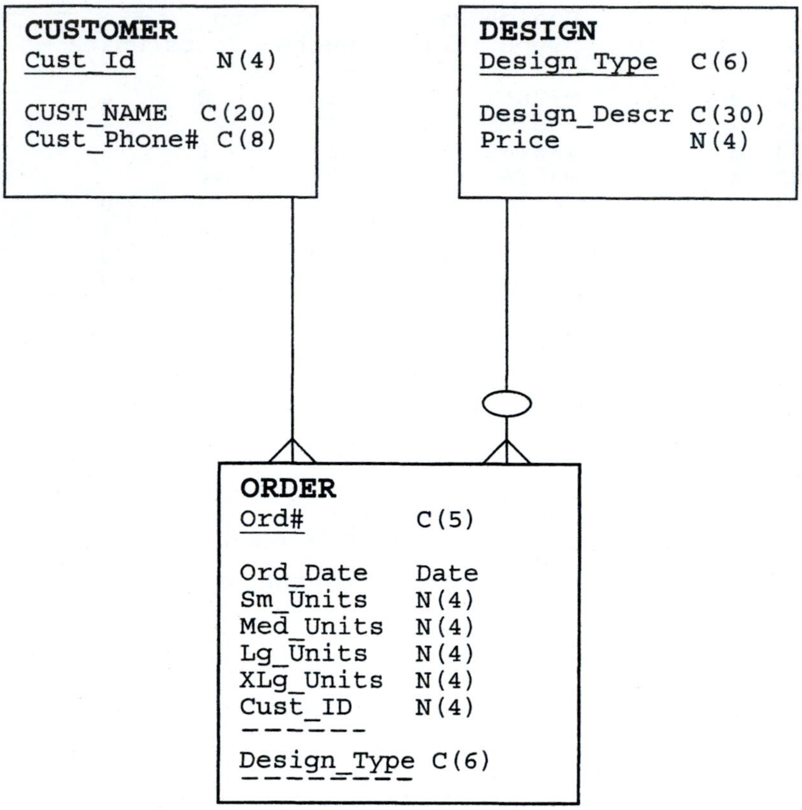

```
CUSTOMER                        DESIGN
Cust_Id       N(4)              Design_Type  C(6)

CUST_NAME  C(20)                Design_Descr C(30)
Cust_Phone# C(8)                Price        N(4)
```

```
ORDER
Ord#          C(5)

Ord_Date      Date
Sm_Units      N(4)
Med_Units     N(4)
Lg_Units      N(4)
XLg_Units     N(4)
Cust_ID       N(4)
- - - - - -
Design_Type C(6)
- - - - - - -
```

REPORTS REVISITED

In a typical database package, most of the computational work for reports can be accomplished in the query that is used as its input. This is illustrated in Figure 5-16 below. The required query links or joins the ORDER, DESIGN, and CUSTOMER tables based on the condition that the value of DESIGN_TYPE is equal between the ORDER and DESIGN tables and the condition that the CUST_ID is equal between the ORDER and CUSTOMER tables. Displayed columns are to include the ORD# and ORD_DATE columns from the ORDER table, the CUST_NAME column of the CUSTOMER table, and the DESIGN_TYPE, DESIGN_DESCRIPTION, and PRICE columns of the DESIGN table. The query would also include a computed field summing the number of shirts of all sizes ordered (=SM_UNITS + MED_UNITS + LG_UNITS + XLG_UNITS) and another computed field to calculate the total amount billed for the order. We are assuming no taxes or other added charges and no volume discounts. Thus, this field will equal (SM_UNITS + MED_UNITS + LG_UNITS + XLG_UNITS)*PRICE. Figure 5-17shows what the results of this query would look like for the sets of sample data shown in Figures 5-12, 5-13, and 5-14.

Figure 5-16
Layout Form for the Billing Summary Report

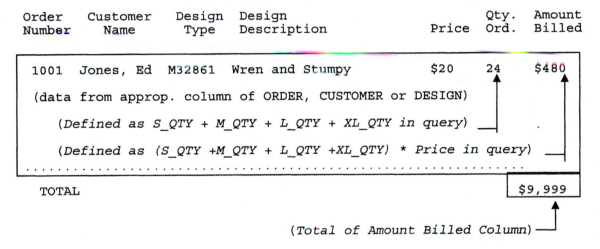

```
DATA SOURCE: Query Linking the ORDER, CUSTOMER and DESIGN Tables

              Summary of Billings for Pending Orders

                                                        Qty.   Amount
Order   Customer   Design  Design                       Ord.   Billed
Number  Name       Type    Description          Price

  1001  Jones, Ed  M32861  Wren and Stumpy      $20     24       $480

(data from approp. column of ORDER, CUSTOMER or DESIGN)

    (Defined as S_QTY + M_QTY + L_QTY + XL_QTY in query)

    (Defined as (S_QTY +M_QTY + L_QTY +XL_QTY) * Price in query)
........................................................................

  TOTAL                                                         $9,999
```

(*Total of Amount Billed Column*)

Figure 5-17
Sample Query Results Linking ORDER, CUSTOMER, and DESIGN Tables

Order Number	Customer's Name	Design Type	Design Description	Price	Qty. Ord.	Amount Billed
1001	Barnes, Janet	M32861	Troubled Toad	$20	24	$ 480
1002	Jones, Ed	CUSTOM	Custom Design	$25	53	$1,325
1003	Adams, Al	R38671	Happy Face	$15	42	$ 630
1004	Davis, Owen	M32861	Troubled Toad	$20	149	$2,980
1005	Barnes, Janet	CUSTOM	Custom Design	$25	20	$ 500
1006	Morris, Sue	P22371	Einstein	$20	28	$ 560
1007	Bates, Nancy	CUSTOM	Custom Design	$25	28	$ 700
1008	Adams, Al	P22371	Einstein	$20	39	$ 780
1009	Date, Charles	R38671	Happy Face	$15	30	$ 450
1010	Evans, Jim	M32861	Troubled Toad	$20	52	$1,040

SUMMARY

Often you will need to choose whether to use a spreadsheet package or database package to develop an application. In other instances you may need to combine the use of a database and a spreadsheet package to produce an integrated application. Each application or application component should be developed using the type of package which best fits the work to be done. In general, database packages are best for handling sets of data that will be generated and maintained over time, used by several users, and used to produce multiple types of reports. Spreadsheet packages are best for ad-hoc, or one shot applications, for applications requiring substantial interaction, i.e. "what-if" analysis, and for applications requiring complex computations.

The analysis stage of an end user application can be documented by an application requirements report. This report is simply a set of brief descriptions of the key output, input, processing, storage, control, and user interface requirements of an application.

For the design phase of application development layout forms similar to those described for spreadsheet applications may be used. However, design of the structure of a database file is best handled by creating a data dictionary form that describes key characteristics of the data and its structure.

Coding of database applications involves at least four elements; creation of one or more database tables, creation of forms for the entry and editing of data, entry of sample data to populate the database, and creation reports to manipulate the stored data and produce desired results.

Testing of database applications has several elements. We must ensure that all reasonable data values are accepted by the system and stored properly, ensure that all computations performed are correct, ensure that data are indexed properly to support reports requiring sorted data, and ensure that all requirements of the system are met.

Database applications generally require more external documentation than their spreadsheet counterparts. Written documentation describing the procedures to be followed by each user of the application should be provided. The level of detail in which procedures are described should be matched to the needs of the user. Particular care should be taken to ensure that control procedures, such as procedures for making back-up copies of the database file, are well documented and fully understood.

The most common type of integrated application is one in which data are collected and stored in a database file and then copied to a spreadsheet file for analysis and display.

Many end user database applications may require the use of multiple related tables. Where this type of structure is needed, related tables are linked based on the value of a common data field that is a unique identifying field in on of the tables. Queries are created to establish these linkages and reports can be produced which are derived from these queries.

CHAPTER 6: DATABASE CASES

🌐 CASE 1: Baxter Turbine

The Baxter Turbine Corporation (BT) is a leading firm in the aerospace industry. Auto-related air pollution and traffic congestion are serious problems in the city where BT's headquarters are located. BT is looked on as a leader in the business community and has always been actively involved in civic improvement activities. For instance, BT has staggered its work schedules to help relieve traffic congestion. Workers can choose from schedule "A" (6 AM to 3 PM) "B" (8:00 AM to 5:00 PM) or schedule "C" (9:30 Am to 6:30 PM). Now BT and other leading businesses have been asked to take measures to encourage car pooling. In order to demonstrate leadership in this area, Evelyn Davis, CEO of the BT Corporation, wants to implement an aggressive car pooling plan within the company.

Ms. Davis wants to encourage employees to form car pools with other BT employees. To assist in the forming of car pools, she wants to distribute data identifying sets of employees living in the same area of town who could potentially form a car pool.

The BT building is located in a congested downtown area. There is a small parking lot (75 car capacity) located under the BT building. Currently, upper level managers are assigned parking in this lot, while all other employees must park in an uncovered lot three blocks away. As an incentive to employees to form car pools, Ms. Davis has decided to convert the parking lot under the building to a car pool lot. Any employee who joins a car pool will be allowed to park under the building. All employees who are not car pool members will be required to park in the uncovered lot. Each car pool member will be issued a parking permit for his/her car. The number on the parking permit will correspond to the number of the assigned parking space. The same sticker number will be assigned to each member of a car pool so that only one vehicle from each car pool will be able to park in the covered lot. A parking lot attendant will periodically monitor the lot to ensure that only cars with the appropriate permit are allowed to park in the covered lot.

Several of the staff members have company cars assigned to them. Ms. Davis wants to insist that staff with assigned cars join a car pool if it is reasonable for them to do so. Employees with assigned cars will be exempted from the requirement to car pool only if car pooling would increase their commuting time by more than 10 minutes, or if their work and travel schedule does not allow them to participate in a car pool.

Ms. Davis assigns you the task of implementing this car pooling scheme. She indicates that you are to prepare a memorandum for her signature to be sent to all employees describing the car pooling program. Attached to this memorandum will be a list of all BT employees and their work schedule and addresses sorted by the prefix (first three digits) of their home phone. Using the first three digits of the seven digit home phone number is seen as the best way to identify sets of workers living in the same general area. Employees are to be asked to identify and contact fellow workers to form car pools. Workers with assigned company cars are to be notified that their continued use of those cars may depend upon joining a car pool. The parking lot under the building is to be converted to car pool use one month from the date of the memo. As employees form car pools, they are to contact you to receive permits for the lot. You are to keep a record of each employee who is issued a permit and the permit number assigned to that employee.

At the end of the one month sign up period, Ms. Davis wants you to send her a list of all employees who have joined a car pool. She also wants to see a list of all employees who have a company car but have not joined a car pool by the implementation date. She plans to have one of her aides personally contact those employees to determine whether they qualify for exemption from the car pooling requirement.

Once the car pooling plan is in place, Ms. Davis wants you to continue to publish lists, by phone number prefix, of employees who are not yet members of a car pool. She wants lists to be distributed at least once a month until enough car pools are formed to fill the parking lot under the building.

To complete the task you have been assigned, you need to know the name, work hours, address, and phone number of each employee. You also need to know whether or not an employee has an assigned company car. As the car pool plan is implemented, you will add data indicating the number of the parking sticker assigned to each employee who joins a car pool. You contact the IS department to determine what data they can provide. They indicate that they can retrieve a set of employee data for you and have it copied to a file for use with the database package on your PC. This file will include the name, work schedule, address (street, city, state and zip code), office phone number, home phone prefix number, and company car status (Yes or No) for each employee. They will generate a sample set of this data for 50 employees for your use in developing your application. You will receive a full, up-to-date employee list when you are ready to implement your system. A sample of this data is shown after the data dictionary form below. The full sample of 50 records is available in an ACCESS file called **Case61_bt.mdb** on your data disk.

You plan to work with the retrieved file and to add a field to store the parking sticker assignments of employees who join car pools. For several reasons, this information will be stored in your personal database and not in the organizational database. First, the car pool plan is experimental and may change over time. Second, you will be the only user of this data, at least initially. Finally, the IS department would be unable to make the necessary changes to place this data in the organizational database within the required time frame. It is quite possible that the parking sticker information you generate may be placed in an organizational database at some future date.

Application Development Notes

Design aids for this application are presented below and a set of sample employee data records are provided for you on your data disk. Before proceeding with this application, you should make a back-up copy of that file.

Your first step for this project should be to access the presupplied database file and modify its structure to include the *sticker_no* column that will store assigned car pool parking sticker numbers. Once this modification has been made, you can proceed to other considerations. You will need to edit some of the data to add car pool sticker numbers for selected employees (as described below) in order to test some of the reports produced by this application. All reports except the first one are based on only selected records from the table. In most PC based database packages, the selection of qualifying records is most easily accomplished by creating a query which applies the selection criteria. That query then becomes the source for the report that is created. Two of the reports require that data be grouped by phone prefix. Remember that those reports will operate correctly only if the report is based on a query that is sorted by phone prefix.

Assignment

1.   Based upon the descriptions above, the supplied database file, and the design documents shown below - develop an application using a database management package which meets all of the requirements described for this case. Test your application for accuracy and completeness. Write an appropriate set of documentation to accompany your application. Your documentation should be designed to support your personal use of the system or use by other individuals who are experienced in the use of database packages.

2.   Make copies of all of the reports generated by this application. To produce meaningful reports for the portion of the application that utilizes car pool sticker data, you will need to assign stickers to some of the employees in the sample database. Pick at least 5 pairs of employees and assign them car pool stickers beginning with the sticker number 01. Make sure that at least two employees who have company cars are included in the set of employees getting car pool stickers.

3.   There are likely to be numerous instances where querying of your database will be required. To demonstrate that your database can handle queries, retrieve the following data from your database:
   A.   A count of the number of employees in car pools,
   B.   The names and phone numbers of the employees who are assigned to parking sticker number 2,
   C.   A list of all available data for employees in phone prefix 813 who are members of a car pool,
   D.   A list of the names and phone numbers of all employees on work schedule C who are not car pool members,
   E.   A count of the number of non carpool members on each work schedule (A, B, and C.

4.   ⑤ Prepare a set of web pages that could be used to promote the car-pooling plan. Your web pages should include at least - A main page that describes the program

and contains links to: A page listing all employees who have signed up for the carpool program and A page listing all employees grouped by phone prefix and Schedule. Your pages should contain appropriate links back to the main page and to important locations within the page, such as, links allowing the user to go to a listing of employees in a particular phone prefix area.

Detailed design specifications for the design of the web pages are not presented here, since a variety of options could be used.

Web pages including database data that is frequently updated or that is based on interactions with the user require dynamic linking between the database and the web page. This type of dynamic linking may not be required when the data to be displayed do not change frequently. Data from a database query can easily be incorporated into a web page by simply copying the query results and then pasting them into your web page design environment. Typically, your web design tool will automatically convert your query results into a table. Thus, it is suggested that you generate set of queries (rather than formal reports) for the data you wish to include in your web pages. Then simply copy the query results to appropriate locations in your web pages. Follow the principles laid out in Chapter 1 with respect to the structure and linkages among your web pages.

Application Requirements Report

OUTPUT REQUIREMENTS

1. A report of employee names, addresses and phone #s grouped by home
   phone prefix.

2. A report of names, addresses, and parking sticker #s of employees who
   have joined a car pool.

3. A report listing the names and office phone #s of employees who have
   a company car but are not car pool members.

4. A report of names, addresses and office phone #s of employees who are
   not yet car pool members, grouped by home phone prefix.

INPUT REQUIREMENTS

All input data except the car pool sticker number will be supplied in a
   file extracted from an organizational database.

Car pool sticker number data are to be assigned when employees sign up
   for a car pool.

PROCESSING REQUIREMENTS

Required processing includes sorting on home phone prefix (1, 4) and
   selecting subsets of the data based on whether an employee has an
   assigned car (3) and/or whether the employee has joined a car pool
   (2, 3, 4).

STORAGE REQUIREMENTS

All data except sticker numbers will be extracted at the beginning of
   implementation. Sticker numbers will be collected as assigned and
   maintained for periodic reporting. Data will be maintained
   indefinitely.

CONTROL / USER INTERFACE REQUIREMENTS

All data entry / corrections / report generation is to be performed by
   the developer or by an individual with substantial prior
   experience with the database package used for development.

Car pool sticker assignments are to be recorded in written form as well
   as being placed in the database file. A back-up copy of the car
   pool database file will be made at the close of each work-week.

Entity Diagram

```
┌─────────────────────────────────────┐
│ CAR POOL                             │
│ Emp_Name              C(15)          │
│ Work_Sched            C(1)           │
│ Street_Add            C(40)          │
│ City                  C(15)          │
│ Zip_Code              C(5)           │
│ Ph_Prefix             C(3)           │
│ Wk_Phone              C(4)           │
│ Co_Car                C(3)           │
│ Sticker_no            C(3)           │
│                                      │
└─────────────────────────────────────┘
```

Sample of Supplied Data

EMP NAME	WORK SCHED	STREET ADDRESS	CITY	ZIP CODE	PHONE PREFIX	WK PHONE	CO CAR
Barnes, Ann	C	1315 N. Tatum	Phoenix	83266	776	2319	No
Barrow, Carl	A	2807 N. 42nd Ave.	Phoenix	83412	753	4118	No
Bowers, Ann	A	1436 N. 52nd Street	Tempe	83418	813	1194	Yes
Boyle, Ann	C	4503 N. Ocotillo	Scottsdale	84082	902	2113	No
Cole, Carla	B	4322 W. Roosevelt	Tempe	83418	813	3674	Yes
Davis, Daniel	C	3814 N. Spruce	Tempe	83418	813	2822	No

Layout Forms

REPORT OF EMPLOYEES BY HOME PHONE PREFIX LOCATION

```
Input Data to        All records of CAR_POOL table sorted
  the Report:        by Ph_Prefix
```

BT Employees Grouped by Home Phone Prefix
for Your use in Finding Potential Car Pooling Opportunities

Employee Name	Work Schedule	Street Address	City	Work Phone Extension #

Phone Prefix: [749] { *Lowest phone prefix Value*

```
Davis, Daniel   B       2146 N. Shea          Phoenix          1623

   (data from the appropriate column of the CAR_POOL table
   -  with the appropriate Ph_Prefix value)
```

Phone Prefix: [XXX] { *Next lowest Phone prefix Value*

```
   (as above - data from the CAR_POOL table - for employees in the
      next phone prefix area)
```

.
.
.

REPORT OF CAR POOL MEMBERSHIP

```
Input Data to      Selected record from CAR_POOL table
  the report:      where Sticker_no is greater than zero
```

Car Pool Membership List

Employee Name	Street Address	City	Car Pool Sticker #

```
Adams, Alvin   1978 Rural Road                 Scottsdale      06

   (data for the appropriate column of the CAR_POOL database
      meeting the selection criterion specified above)

XXXXXXXXXXXXXX XXXXXXXXXXXXXXXXXXXXXXXXXXXX  XXXXXXXXXXXXXX XX
```

REPORT OF NON CAR POOL MEMBERS HAVING COMPANY CARS

Input Data to   Selected records from CAR_POOL table
  The Report: where Co_Car = Yes and Sticker_No
                   Is not greater than zero.

               List of Employees Who Have Company Vehicles
                     And Are Not Yet Car Pool Members

```
            Employee                      Work Phone
              Name                        Extension #
         ┌──────────────────────────────────────────────┐
         │ Davis, Daniel                      1623        │
         │                                                │
         │  (data for the appropriate column             │
         │  of the CAR_POOL table meeting                │
         │  the selection criteria specified)            │
         │                                                │
         │ XXXXXXXXXXXXXXXX                   XXXX         │
         └──────────────────────────────────────────────┘
```

REPORT OF NON CAR POOL MEMBERS BY HOME PHONE PREFIX LOCATION

Input Data to   Selected records from CAR_POOL table
  The Report: Sticker_No is not greater than zero,
                   Sorted by Ph_prefix.

                  List of BT Employees who are not Currently
                          Car Pool Members

```
┌───────────────────────────────────────────────────────────────┐
│ The design of the body of this report is identical to that of  │
│ the REPORT OF EMPLOYEES BY HOME PHONE PREFIX LOCATION on prior  │
│ page.                                                           │
└───────────────────────────────────────────────────────────────┘
```

CASE 2: Al's Affordable Autos

Al Fields is the owner of Al's Affordable Autos, an independent used car dealership. Al purchases used vehicles at auto auctions, through agreements with several new car dealerships, and as trade-ins or direct purchases from private individuals. As the name of Al's business implies, he specializes in older lower-priced vehicles. For the most part, Al's Affordable Autos sales are either to households looking for a second or third car or to low income households. Al operates strictly on a cash purchase basis, although he has a working agreement with a local finance company, which provides financing to many of Al's customers.

Al has a staff of five salespersons. His sales staff are paid a small salary, but the bulk of their income comes from commissions. The commission has two components. The first component is a percentage of the sales price of the vehicle. This commission rate is negotiated and varies across the sales staff. Generally, Al starts new salespersons with a small commission with the promise to raise the commission rate if they prove to be effective and remain with the firm. The second component is a commission on the mark-up on a vehicle. Mark-up is determined as the difference between dealer cost and the sales price. Dealer cost is recorded as the amount Al paid for a vehicle. In the case of trade-ins, the dealer cost recorded is Al's estimate of the vehicle's wholesale value. Prices in this industry are very much subject to negotiation. All sales negotiated by the sales staff must be approved by Al. Al feels that it is necessary to base much of his sales staff's commissions on the mark-up on the cars they sell. This reduces their incentive to squeeze Al's profit margin in order to make a sale. This commission on mark-up is the same for all salespersons, 10 percent.

Micki Stephens has served as Al's secretary and bookkeeper for 12 years. All records have been kept in manual form. However, the scale of operations has expanded substantially in recent years to the point where it has become very difficult for Micki to keep the books up to date. Two years ago, Micki took an introductory computing course at a local community college. Since that time, she has been pressuring Al to buy a PC so that some of her work can be computerized. Recently, Al accepted a used PC with accompanying software as a trade-in. He now wants to begin computerizing his records. Micki suggests that they begin by creating a file to record summary information about the stock of cars on the lot and sales of those cars. This information could be used to keep track of Al's inventory of vehicles. It could also calculate commissions due to each employee. Micki believes that a database package could be used to develop this type of application. She does not feel that she knows enough about database software to construct such an application. However, she does feel confident that she could operate an application of this type once it has been developed. Al asks you to develop this application for him.

You begin discussions with Al and Micki to determine the requirements for this system. Al indicates that he would like to be able to get a weekly listing of his inventory of vehicles. He'd like that listing to be sorted on the make of car so he can see if he has "too many Chevys and not enough Fords." This information would help him decide which cars to bid on at the auto auctions he attends. Al also indicates that he'd like to be able to retrieve a list of the cars in stock of a particular make and model. This would help him respond to telephone calls from customers interested in a particular type of vehicle.

Micki is primarily interested in being able to use the computer to compute commissions. Commissions are paid monthly and are based on the commission rates described above.

As you discuss the specifics of data collection with Micki, you find that data about each vehicle are recorded at two distinct times. First, descriptive information is recorded at the time Al's Affordable Autos purchases a vehicle. This information includes the make, model, and year of the vehicle and its vehicle identification number. Also recorded are the date of the purchase and the price Al paid for the vehicle (dealer cost). Several other items about the vehicle are also recorded at this time, but Micki feels that only the items described above need to be included in the database initially.

Additional information is recorded when a vehicle is sold. This information includes the sale date, the sales price, the salesperson's name, and the purchaser's name. Micki notes that it is important to record the purchaser's name and have it print out on the report that calculates commissions. The sales staff keep track of their sales by the name of their customers and they will want to check to make sure that they get credit for all of their sales. In fact, she notes that salespersons frequently inquire about a specific sale to make sure that they have been credited for it. Also, it is necessary to know the salesperson's commission rate in order to calculate their commission accurately. She has done this from memory in the past, but assumes that the commission rate will now be stored in the database.

Micki and Al indicate that Micki will be the only direct user of the system. She will enter the data, generate the reports, and pull out any ad-hoc information needed by Al and the sales staff. Micki has some prior experience with the database package you are using and is confident that she will be able to handle these tasks.

Micki is able to supply you with a small set of sample data for your use in developing this application. The sample data have been selected from cars sold over the past six weeks and cars currently in inventory, and are shown below.

Application Development Notes

Analysis and design documents for this application are shown below. After reviewing these documents, your first step in development of this application should be to create a table documenting the structure indicated in the data dictionary form. Because the creation of the database file structure is a part of your assignment, no computerized data file is provided for this assignment. After you have created your database file, you should populate it with the sample data. The indexes required to sort the data for reporting must be created and maintained before the reports are produced. Finally, the required reports should be created and tested, incorporating the calculations and summary operations described in the layout form.

Al's Affordable Autos Sales and Inventory Sample Data

Make	Model	Year	Vehicle ID No.	Purchase Date	Dealer Cost	Sales Date	Spsn. Id	Customer Name	Sales Price
Chevy	Malibu	1996	163217	09/06/04	$2,050	10/03/04	1	Smith R.	$2,775
Pont.	Grand Am	1992	234BT8	09/10/04	$1,000				$0
Ford	Taurus	1994	483492	09/12/04	$2,325	10/18/04	2	Jones, J.	$2,962
Ford	Escort	1999	782391	09/14/04	$2,000				$0
Buick	Regal	1990	2183J9	09/14/04	$1,460	10/15/04	4	Fox, T.	$1,950
Pont.	Grand Am	1992	318BT6	09/15/04	$2,175				$0
Chevy	Malibu	1990	0936I2	09/17/04	$715	09/24/04	1	Thomas, R.	$975
Honda	Civic	1993	274381	09/18/04	$1,725	10/08/04	3	Robb, J.	$2,287
Dodge	Colt	1989	33J829	09/18/04	$560				$0
Ford	Taurus	1994	472386	09/21/04	$3,185	10/24/04	2	Owens, P.	$4,200
Pont.	Grand Am	1991	279BT2	09/21/04	$2,135	10/19/04	3	Fell, R.	$2,512
Ford	Taurus	1993	624918	09/26/04	$1,950				$0
Dodge	Colt	1991	64J397	09/26/04	$1,575	10/08/04	1	Wells, D.	$1,950
Ford	Escort	1993	184935	09/28/04	$1,800				$0
Honda	Civic	1992	392763	09/28/04	$2,175				$0
Chevy	Malibu	1989	389724	09/30/04	$675	10/19/04	4	Morris, V.	$900
Dodge	Colt	1993	53J935	10/02/04	$1,650				$0
Ford	Taurus	1994	284692	10/04/04	$1,950	10/27/04	3	Baker, H.	$2,730
Honda	Civic	1991	307B92	10/06/04	$1,500	10/28/04	2	Dowd, P.	$1,895
Dodge	Colt	1994	58J839	10/11/04	$1,725				$0
Buick	Regal	1992	394871	10/11/04	$1,985	10/24/04	2	Allen, G.	$2,760

Al's Affordable Autos Salesperson Commission Data

Salesperson ID	Salesperson Name	Commission Rate
1	Adams, Jack	1.50%
2	Davis, Randy	2.00%
3	Lewis, Lynn	1.75%
4	Bates, Bev	1.50%

Assignment

1.   Based upon the data supplied and the analysis and design reports and forms
      provided below, develop a database application to fulfill all of the requirements of
      this case. Test your application for accuracy and completeness. Produce a set of
      printed reports based upon your sample data.

2.   Write an appropriate set of documentation to accompany your application. Be sure
      that your documentation will fully describe all of the procedures Micki needs to
      follow including procedures for control and security of the database.

3.   Prepare a set of presentation materials to be used to demonstrate your application's
      main features to Al and Micki. These materials should demonstrate how the
      system works and summarize the key procedures they will need to use to operate
      it effectively.

4.   To ensure that your application can accommodate the kinds of ad-hoc queries that
      are likely to be needed, execute the following queries based on your sample data:

      A. Retrieve a list of all Ford Taurus that are in Al's inventory
      B. Retrieve all available information about the car sold to "Thomas, R." , including
          the amount of commission paid.
      C. Retrieve the total dealer cost for all vehicles in Al's Affordable Autos's inventory
          whose make is Ford.
      D. Retrieve the total sales price and total of commissions paid on all sales of cars
          whose make is Ford.

Application Requirements Report

OUTPUT REQUIREMENTS

A report of inventory of cars sorted by model is to be produced weekly.

A report of sales commissions is to be produced monthly. This report must show data for each sale made by a salesperson as well as a total commission earned for the month for each salesperson.

Support should be provided for ad-hoc retrievals of data about cars in inventory with selected features or data about recently sold cars meeting selected criteria. Selections are likely to be based on Make, Model, or Year of car or upon the salesperson or customer name for vehicles that have been sold.

INPUT REQUIREMENTS

All input data are to be recorded by Micki Stephens. Inventory data will be recorded at the time a car is purchased by Al's Affordable Autos. Sales information will be recorded as each vehicle is sold.

A Salesperson table containing the salesperson's name and their commission rate is to be maintained. This table is needed to calculate commissions properly for the monthly commission report.

PROCESSING REQUIREMENTS

Required processing for report 1 includes selecting vehicles (from the INV_SALE table) that have not been sold and sorting on Model type.

Required processing for report 2 includes selecting data from INV_SALE for vehicles sold in the correct month joined with the SALESPERSON to get the associated commission rate, sorting and grouping data by salesperson, and calculating the commission earned for each sale and total commission earned by each salesperson.

STORAGE REQUIREMENTS

Car inventory data are to be collected as cars are purchased and updated as each car is sold. Data will be stored for periodic reporting. Data on vehicles sold will be kept in the database until at least 60 days after the sale date.

The salesperson table is maintained indefinitely and updated as needed.

CONTROL / USER INTERFACE REQUIREMENTS

All database operations (data entry, data correction and deletion, report generation, database querying, and back-up of the database) are to be performed exclusively by Micki Stephens.

A back-up copy of the inventory and sales tables is to be made by Micki Stephens at the close of each work day.

Entity Relationship Diagram

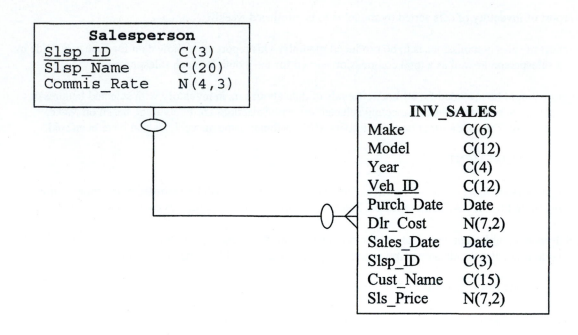

Layout Forms

INVENTORY REPORT

Input Data to   Selected data from INV_SALE for vehicles not yet
   the Report: sold (SALES_PRICE < 1) sorted by Model

Al's Affordable Autos Used Vehicle Inventory

Make	Model	Model Year	Vehicle Id Number	Date Purchased	Dealer Cost
Pont.	Bonneville	1983	M18734LV27	09/10/96	675.00
Pont.	Bonneville	1986	R19268Mr18	09/15/96	1850.00

(data from the appropriate column sorted in
alphabetical order by model)

Total   (col. tot.)

SALES COMMISSION REPORT

Input data to   Selected data from INV_SALE joined with
   The report: SALESPERSON for vehicles sold in the
                     target month sorted by salesperson name

Monthly Commission Report

Make	Model	Model Year	Customer Name	Date Sold	Dealer Cost	Sales Price	Commission Earned
		Salesperson: Adams, J.	*1st value of salesperson name*				
Chevy	Nova	1985	Smith, R.	10/03/96	675.00	850.00	34.50

(data from the appropriate column of the INV_SALE database   computed
for this salesperson)   field *

Subtotal   col. sub total

Salesperson: Xxxxx, X.   *Next value of Salesperson name*

         .   .   .   .   .
         .   .   .   .   .
         .   .   .   .   .

Total   gr. tot. of col.

*   *computed commission field = Sls_Price * Comm_rate +*
     *(Sls_Price - Dlr_Cost) * .1*

CASE 3: Lake Country Music Supply

Lake Country Music Supply sells musical instruments to retail customers and provides tune-up and repair services. Frank Barnes, owner of Lake Country Music Supply believes that tune-up and repair services are a key selling point. He cannot match the prices offered by internet and mail-order suppliers, but he has been able to retain a strong customer base by being a full service supplier. To drive home the advantages offered by buying lawn equipment from them, Metropolitan offers a year of free service and repair with each new instrument they sell.

Currently, information about the instruments that have been sold is maintained manually. However, Frank would like to have a computer application that would allow him to retrieve key information about each instrument Metropolitan has sold, and he has asked you to develop it for him. Frank would like to have an application that would allow him to do three key things:

1. Look up information about any instrument when a customer brings it in. The information provided should include the purchase date and the date of the last servicing performed on the instrument. This would allow Frank to quickly determine if an instrument is under the one-year service and repair agreement.

2. Retrieve a list of names and addresses of customers whose year of free servicing expires soon (within three months) who have not yet had their instrument serviced. Bob feels that sending a reminder to these customers will help to build goodwill and may also get them in the habit of using his service department.

4. Retrieve a list of names and phone numbers of customers whose last instrument servicing was more than ten months ago. This list would be retrieved when business was slow in the service department. The customers identified would be called and offered a discount if they brought their instrument in for service within a two week period. Bob feels that this would help to eliminate slack periods in the service department, and would also improve goodwill with customers.

While a substantial amount of information could be collected about each instrument sold, Frank wants to keep the data collection as simple as possible. Data are recorded by Frank's sales staff, and many of them have no prior experience in the use of computers. Frank believes that the set of data collected for each purchase should include: the name of the purchaser, the type of instrument, the model and identification number of the instrument, and the date the instrument was sold. When an instrument is serviced, Frank wants to record the date that the servicing was completed.

Frank indicates that he also maintains information about customers on a set of index cards. The information he needs is just their name, street address, and phone number. He suggests that this file should also be computerized.

As you ask Frank Barnes additional questions, you find out several important details. Some customers may have purchased several instruments from Metropolitan. Also there are a few instances where two of Frank's customers have the same name. You suggest using a Customer ID field to link customers to their instruments. Frank is hesitant because of concerns about becoming less friendly in dealings with customers. You assure him that the system can be built to allow customers to get services without having to remember their customer number.

You also discover that, only information about the most recent servicing is needed. When an instrument is serviced for the second time, the date of the second servicing can simply replace that of the first servicing in the database. Finally, you discover that there is a five character model code for each type of instrument that uniquely identifies the manufacturer and model and that the identification number for an instrument is a unique code of up to ten characters.

Frank indicates that he will personally retrieve the lists of customers for servicing and for discount offers as needed. He suggests that the lists should include the model and identification number of the instrument and the date of sale (or servicing) as well as the customer's name and address (or phone number). Frank and two of his employees have enough experience with spreadsheet packages to perform ad-hoc queries. When it is necessary to retrieve the record for an individual instrument or to perform some other ad-hoc retrieval, one of them will be available. To help you develop your application, Frank was able to provide you with the sample set of data shown below.

Application Development Notes

Sample data and a set of analysis and design documents for this application are provided below. Before developing this application you should read all of this documentation carefully. The first step in implementing the application design will be to create a database file whose structure corresponds to the descriptions in the data dictionary form. Once the structure of your database file has been created, you will need to create appropriate data entry forms and input the records for the set of sample data shown. When the data have been entered, you can create the two reports required for this application, using the layout forms provided as a guide. *To test your application using the sample data, assume that the current date is the first day of November, 2004 (11/01/04).*

Assignment

1.   Using the sample data and design documents provided, develop a database application that will meet all of the requirements described for this case. Be sure to test your application for completeness and accuracy.

2.   Produce a set of presentation materials that could be used to describe your application and procedures for using it to Frank and his staff.

3.   Write a set of documentation to accompany this application. Your documentation should appropriately describe the procedures to be followed by all users of the system and should describe control and backup procedures to be followed.

4.   To test your application's capabilities to support queries, perform the following query operations on the sample data and get printed listings of your results:
      A.   Get a list of the names, addresses, and phone numbers of customers buying model MC620,
      B.   Find the ID number of the Clarinet bought by "Warren, Wayne",
      C.   Get a listing of the names and phone numbers of customers who bought Clarinets.

Lake Country Music Supply Sample Data

INSTRUMENT					
Instrument ID	Instrument Type	Model	Sales Date	Customer ID	Last Service Date
00748A2639	Trumpet	MC680	8/17/2002	10	11/14/2003
00748A2659	Saxophone	MC620	9/5/2003	11	
01023A7413	Trombone	MC470	9/23/2001	12	12/7/2003
01328A3914	Clarinet	MC270	11/13/2003	13	
01386B7106	Saxophone	MC620	6/2/2001	14	4/22/2002
016V219	Clarinet	JR480	9/18/2003	11	
01863A8327	Clarinet	MC270	7/7/2001	10	12/14/2003
02314A2861	Trombone	MC470	11/23/2003	16	
0238V813	Trumpet	JR690	6/5/2002	13	4/21/2004
0316V248	Trumpet	JR690	5/25/2002	18	11/17/2003
0566V791	Trumpet	JR690	7/2/2002	19	
1307283497	Saxophone	ST190	12/14/2003	20	5/6/2004
1427306297	Trumpet	ST290	4/8/2002	10	
1672934107	Tuba	ST390	12/31/2003	21	
2178309725	Trumpet	ST280	10/17/2003	22	
2372B724	Trumpet	JR690	11/29/2003	23	12/23/2003
273645924	Trombone	MC470	12/29/2003	17	
2864B018	Clarinet	JR480	6/12/2002	21	10/8/2004
3648B824	Flute	JR220	5/18/2004	21	
3701723648	Trumpet	ST280	11/4/2003	24	
3816824083	Trumpet	ST280	6/25/2001	25	
4913059214	Trumpet	ST280	10/27/2000	17	7/4/2002
8140286437	Tuba	ST390	6/8/2003	26	3/13/2004

Customers			
Customer Id	Customer Name	Street Address	Phone Number
10	Warren, Wayne	1404 Elm St.	551-9271
11	Owens, Jim	907 Market St.	768-1098
12	Hall, Mark	1776 Washington Rd.	526-9110
13	Ward, Walter	2411 Maple St.	736-4813
14	Allen, Bob	2101 N. Poplar St.	762-1913
16	Graves, Dan	392 Main St.	776-9208
17	Clay, Art	244 Maple St.	768-2464
18	Howell, Hal	2104 S. Poplar	541-6824
19	Morris, Marie	823 Elm St.	527-4819
20	Dale, Dan	2604 Adams Rd.	773-0291
21	Bailey, Al	1426 Lincoln rd.	773-8205
22	Evans, John	412 Lost Lane	541-0037
23	Thomas, Tina	428 Market St.	548-2106
24	Pearson, Bill	1411 Adams Rd.	772-1936
25	Barnett, Ed	814 Lincoln Rd.	521-1203
26	Jarvis, Dale	1102 Elm St.	771-0924

Entity Relationship Diagram

CUSTOMER

Cust_ID	N(4)
Cust_Name	C(20)
Str_Address	C(30)
Phone_No	C(8)

INSTRUMENT

Instrument_ID	C(10)
Instrument_Type	C(8)
Model	C(5)
Sale_date	Date
Cust_ID	N(4)
Service_Date	Date

Application Requirements Report

OUTPUT REQUIREMENTS

1. A report of customer information for instruments sold more than 9 months and less than one year ago.

2. A report of customer information for customers with instruments that was last serviced more than 10 months ago.

3. Support should be provided for ad-hoc retrievals based on customer name, instrument identification number, sale or service date, instrument type, or model number.

INPUT REQUIREMENTS

All input data are to be obtained by sales staff as each sale is made.

PROCESSING REQUIREMENTS

Required processing includes selecting data based on the values of selected fields.

STORAGE REQUIREMENTS

Input data are to be collected as each sale is made and are to be stored for periodic and ad-hoc reporting. Data for each sale and customer will be retained indefinitely.

The service date is to be updated by the service staff each time servicing is performed.

CONTROL / USER INTERFACE REQUIREMENTS

Sales staff are to enter data for new sales only.

Service staff are to modify only the service date for instruments they service.

All corrections to data, report generation, and querying of the database is to be performed by Frank Barnes or other designated employees with experience in the use of database software.

A back-up copy of this data file is to be made by Frank Barnes or a designated employee at the close of business each day.

Layout Forms

Customer Maintenance Form

Used to add new customers and record changes to customer data

```
┌──────────────────────────────────────────┐
│        Add / Edit Customer Form            │
│                                            │
│   Id #        ┌──────┐  Name ┌───────────┐ │
│               │   99 │       │Xxxxx, Xxxx│ │
│               └──────┘       └───────────┘ │
│                                            │
│   Street Address  ┌────────────────────┐   │
│                   │Xxxxx Xxxxxxx Xxx    │   │
│                   └────────────────────┘   │
│                                            │
│   Phone #         ┌────────────────────┐   │
│                   │999-9999            │   │
│                   └────────────────────┘   │
└──────────────────────────────────────────┘
```

Sales and Servicing Form

Used to record new sales and to record date of servicing performed

```
┌──────────────────────────────────────────────┐
│       Instrument Sales / Service Form          │
│                                                │
│  Customer:  ┌──────────────────────┐           │
│             │99  Xxxxx, Xxxx  |>    │           │
│             └──────────────────────┘           │
│                                                │
│  Instrument:                                   │
│                                                │
│     Type:   ┌──────────┐   Model ┌───────┐     │
│             │Xxxxxxxx  │         │XX999  │     │
│             └──────────┘         └───────┘     │
│                                                │
│     Id #    ┌──────────────────────┐           │
│             │          9999999999  │           │
│             └──────────────────────┘           │
│                                                │
│  Sales Date ┌──────────┐                       │
│             │mm/dd/yy  │                       │
│             └──────────┘                       │
│                                                │
│          Last Service Date: ┌──────────┐       │
│                             │mm/dd/yy  │       │
│                             └──────────┘       │
└──────────────────────────────────────────────┘
```

NOTE: The drop down box shown for Customer information on the above form is designed to allow the user to see the customer's name, as well as, their ID #. Only the ID # is mapped to the instruments sold table.

Report of Customers to Contact for Initial Servicing Reminders

```
Input Data to          Selected data from joining the Instrument
  the Report:          and CUSTOMER tables for sales more than 9 months
                       and less than 1 year ago whose
                       service date is null.

        List of Customers to Contact for Equipment Servicing

                                    Instrument            Equip.      Date
Customer Name      Address          Type       Model      Id#         Sold
```

```
Ward, Walter     2411 Maple St.  Clarinet    MC270   00748A2659   11/13/03


  (data from the appropriate column of the query described above)


Xxxxx, Xxxxx       XXXXXXXXXXXXXX XXXXXXX     XXXXX   XXXXXXXXXX   mm/dd/yy
```

Report of Customers for Servicing Discount Offers

```
Input Data to          Selected data from joining the INSTRUMENT and
  the Report:          CUSTOMER tables and selecting instruments whose
                       last service data is more than 10 months ago,
                       but is not null

        List of Customers to Contact for Equipment Servicing
                        Discount Offers

                   Phone   Instrument            Equip.      Date
Customer Name      Number  Type       Model      Id#         Serviced
```

```
Allen, Bob       762-1913 Saxophone MC620     1386B7106   04/22/02


  (data from the appropriate column of the query described above)


Xxxxxxxxxxxxxxx   XXX-XXXX XXXXXXXXX XXXXX    XXXXXXXXXX   mm/dd/yy
```

CASE 4: A1 Parts

This is an integrated case. Data are collected and stored in a database. The database data are copied to a spreadsheet file when calculations better supported by a spreadsheet package are required.

Stan Moore is foreman of the Starter Assembly Department at A1 Parts Company. His department assembles automobile starters that are designed to be used as replacement parts in a in a variety cars and small trucks. The Starter Assembly Department operates 3 shifts 5 days a week, and employs 4 production lines on each shift. Each production line requires 8 workers. When a line worker is absent a substitute worker is used. These substitute workers (subs) come from a pool of new workers who fill-in in various departments. Because of their lack of experience, production generally falls when subs are used.

An inspector randomly inspects 50 units produced by each line on each shift and records the number of defective units found. At the end of each shift, the inspector also records the total number of units produced by each line. The inspector for each shift turns in a Daily Production Slip like the one on the next page.

At the end of each week Ann Dowd, Stan's secretary, must tabulate the total number of units produced by each line and the number of defective units that were found. These weekly totals are recorded on a Production Report that is sent to the Accounting department. The accounting department converts this weekly data into computerized form and uses it to process payroll and to produce management reports. Samples of the Daily Production Slip, and the Production Report, are shown below.

Stan has become concerned by a decline in the productivity of his department over the last several weeks. Stan's own observation and conversations with shift supervisors have lead him to suspect that there may be problems of absenteeism and low productivity on certain shifts on certain days of the week. He also feels that the posting of summaries of the productivity of each shift on a weekly basis might generate a healthy competition between the shifts which could improve morale and output. He has talked to the inspectors for each shift and they have agreed to add a notation of the number of "Sub" workers used on each line to the summary information they turn in on the daily production slip.

Sample Documents: A1 Parts Starter Assembly Department

DAILY PRODUCTION SLIP

Inspector: A. Davis
Shift: Eve
Date: 10/17/04

Line	Units Assembled	Rejected Units	Subs Used
A	1268	2	0
B	1254	0	0
C	1360	4	0
D	1288	5	0

WEEKLY PRODUCTION REPORT

PRODUCTION REPORT
Department: Starter Assembly
Week of (Monday): 10/15/04

Line	Units Assembled	Rejected Units
Day A	6272	17
Day B	6210	10
Day C	6284	13
...	...	...
Ngt D	6548	13

A personal computer has been installed in Stan's office He has acquired an introductory level of knowledge in the use of a popular spreadsheet package. His secretary Ann has learned enough about this spreadsheet package to key in data, but has very limited knowledge of how to manipulate spreadsheets.

Stan believes that he needs an application that will do the following things:

1.   record production information for each line on a daily basis.

2.   produce a summary report which can be used to compare performance across shifts and days of the week on a weekly basis.

3.   automatically total the production information for each line at week's end and produce the Production Report that must be sent to the accounting department.

Stan began working on this application several weeks ago. He got as far as creating a database file and has had Ann enter the data for the most recent week into that file. However, Stan believes that he does not have the time or the skills needed to complete this application. He has asked you to complete the design and development of this application for him. If you are successful, he plans to use this application every week. He will have Ann input the daily production data, while Stan himself plans to print out the weekly reports.

Application Development Notes

A sample of the set of data covering the most recently completed week is shown below. The full set of data for this week is available in the form of an ACCESS database called **case64_A1.mdb** on the web site for this book. Also shown below are: an application requirements report, a diagram of the major components of this application, a data dictionary form, and a set of layout forms. Note that there are several components to this application. Data are to be stored in a database file.

Sample Hours and Production Input data

Starter Assembly				
Line	Prod Date	Subs Used	Units Produced	Reject Units
Day A	10/17/2004	0	1126	7
Day C	10/17/2004	1	1196	3
Day B	10/17/2004	2	1188	4
Eve C	10/17/2004	0	1360	4
Ngt A	10/17/2004	0	1354	2
Ngt D	10/17/2004	0	1404	3
...	...	...	...	...

The weekly production report to the accounting department can be generated as a report using database software. However, the report comparing performance across shifts and days requires calculations that cannot be easily handled by a database package. Therefore, data from the database file are copied to spreadsheet format. The copied data serves as the input area for a spreadsheet application that produces the performance comparison report.

Assignment

1. Using the database file and analysis and design documents provided, develop an integrated application to meet Stan Moore's requirements as described above. Be sure to test your application for accuracy and completeness. Add a documentation section to the spreadsheet portion of your application to make it as self-documenting as possible.

2. Write an appropriate set of documentation to accompany your application. Be sure that your documentation fully describes all of the procedures needed to operate the application.

3. Create a set of presentation materials suitable for presenting your results to Stan and his secretary. These materials should cover procedures for maintaining the database using it to update the spreadsheet portion of the application.

4.   Is the problem described in this case better handled as an integrated application or by using spreadsheet software alone? Write a short paper discussing the advantages and disadvantages of alternative ways of handling this application.

Application Requirements Report

OUTPUT REQUIREMENTS

1. Weekly totals of subs used, units produced, and reject units for each line to be submitted to the accounting department.

2. Summary report of performance by day and by shift produced weekly for distribution and analysis.

INPUT REQUIREMENTS

All input data to come from daily production slips submitted by inspectors. Data will be input on a daily basis.

PROCESSING REQUIREMENTS

Summarization of detail data to produce weekly totals by shift for production, and reject units (1).

Summarization of data to produce averages and comparisons to average by shift and by day (2).

STORAGE REQUIREMENTS

Data has no immediate use in other applications. Data will be maintained in the database for possible future use.

CONTROL / USER INTERFACE REQUIREMENTS

Line performance data are sensitive and should be available only to those who need to know. A backup copy of the data should be made each week when data entry has been completed and checked.

The data entry portion of this application will be accessed on a repeated basis by a novice user. Other portions of the application will be operated by a user with intermediate level computer skills.

Entity Diagram

STARTER_ASSEMBLY	
Line_ID	C(5)
Prod_Date	Date
Subs_Used	N(2)
Units_Prod	N(5)
Reject_Units	N(3)

Application Components for Integrated Implementation

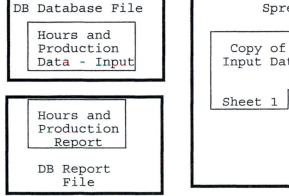
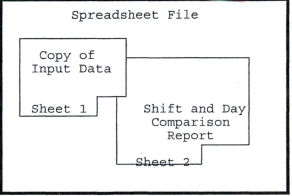

DB Database File

Hours and Production Data - Input

Hours and Production Report

DB Report File

Spreadsheet File

Copy of Input Data

Sheet 1

Shift and Day Comparison Report

Sheet 2

Layout Forms

Starter Assembly Production Form

Used to enter production information on a daily basis and
Modify production records as necessary.

Starter Production Form

Line ID	Production Date	Subs Used	Units Produced	Reject Units
Day A	10/15/04	2	589	6
Xxx X	mm/dd/yy	999	99999	999
.	.	.	.	.
.	.	.	.	.
.	.	.	.	.

Weekly Production Report

Input data to
    the Report: Selected data from Starter Assembly Table
                for the current week.

Weekly Production by Line

Line ID	Units Produced	Reject Units
Xxxxx	99999	999
Xxxxx	99999	999
(Copied from input area	(computed field, sum of Mon_Prod through Fri_Prod 99999	(computed field sum of Mon_Rej through Fri_Rej 999

Spreadsheet Input Area: Daily Hours and Production Data

Line_ID	PROD_DATE	SUBS	PROD	REJ
Day A	10/17/04	1	1053	7

(Data for all days of the week for all three
shifts for the week indicated. This spreadsheet
data area is to be produced by copying the
appropriate data from a query on the database
to this area of your spreadsheet file.)

Ngt E	10/17/04	9	9999	9

Shift and Day Comparison Report Area:

Summary Shift and Day Comparison Report

	Mon.	Tue.	Wed.	Thur.	Fri.	Week-to-date
UNITS PRODUCED						
Day Shift	99999	99999	99999	99999	99999	99999
Evening Shift	(sum of units produced by shift on day					(sum of daily
Night Shift	from cells in the input data area)					shift tots.)
Average	(average across the three shifts)					

UNITS PRODUCED AS A PERCENTAGE OF AVERAGE

Day Shift	999.9%	999.9%	. . .			999.9%
Evening Shift	(shift value divided by average)					
Night Shift	.	.	.	.	.	.

REJECT UNITS

	Mon.	Tue.	Wed.	Thur.	Fri.	Week-to-date
Day Shift	999	999	999	999	999	9999
Evening Shift	(sum of reject units by shift on day					(sum of daily
Night Shift	from cells in the input data area)					shift tots.)
Average	(average across the three shifts)					

REJECT UNITS AS A PERCENTAGE OF AVERAGE

Day Shift	999.9%	999.9%	. . .			999.9%
Evening Shift	(shift value divided by average)					
Night Shift	.	.	.	.	.	.

CASE 5: Pasta by Louisa

Pasta by Louisa is a regional producer and distributor of a refrigerated pasta product. Specifically, Pasta by Louisa produces is a spinach and cheese ravioli made from a special recipe using a carefully guarded process. Pasta by Louisa's product competes as an upscale, quick preparation time, food. By refrigerating its product Pasta by Louisa is able to offer a flavor very close to fresh made pasta with much shorter preparation time. Pasta by Louisa distributes only this one product which it sells exclusively to supermarkets.

Pasta by Louisa's product is vacuum sealed in a plastic. Freshness is an important consideration for consumers. So, to insure freshness, each package of pasta is imprinted with a sales suspension date. Packages not sold by this date are returned to the warehouse to be given to local soup kitchens or destroyed. The suspension dating policy that Pasta by Louisa uses gives their product an effective shelf life of only two weeks.

Louisa Andrews, founder and President of Pasta by Louisa is concerned that sales and stockage information is not being used effectively enough at the supermarket level by individual salespersons. She feels that salespersons are stocking some stores too heavily leading to product having to be destroyed. Even when the suspension date is not reached, pasta on the shelves that is near its suspension date tends to discourage purchases. Excessive stockage also increases Pasta by Louisa's inventory holding costs.

An even bigger problem is the fact that some supermarkets are inadequately stocked with Pasta by Louisa. Salespersons are often required to make emergency restocks of these stores disrupting sales routes and, more importantly, at some stores outages may occur without the Pasta by Louisa salesperson being notified.

Pasta by Louisa salespersons can reduce stockage to stores with lagging sales on their own initiative. However, stockage can be increased only with the approval of the supermarket manager. Supermarket display space is a precious resource since expanded display space tends to spur additional sales.

Ms. Andrews would like to be able to provide each salesperson with the information they need to manage their stockage more effectively. She wants to provide her sales staff with reports showing recent trends in stockage level, sales, and the rate at which the stockage (or inventory) is turned over for each store they serve. The sales staff could use these reports to cut back stockage at stores with lagging sales and to help make the case for increased display space at stores where inventory turnover is high.

The profit margin to supermarkets on the sales of Pasta by Louisa is substantially higher than that for standard national brands. Supermarket managers tend to think of Pasta by Louisa as a low turnover specialty item requiring a higher profit margin and only a minimal amount of shelf space. Ms. Andrews feels that sales statistics for Pasta by Louisa justify increased display space in many stores. She would like to provide each salesperson with a portable PC and an application that would allow them to share information about a store's sales with that store's manager. She feels that reports and graphics presenting sales data directly to store managers in computerized form would be a particularly effective way to persuade them to expand the display space assigned to Pasta by Louisa. She envisions an application that would allow a store manager to see trends in sales, stockage, and the inventory turnover rate for their store. The salesperson could even access the data to do ad-hoc querying or to perform calculations to respond to specific questions a store manager might pose.

The data needed for this application are available in an organizational database maintained by the IS staff. Ms. Andrews expects the application you develop to periodically download summary data from this organizational database into a separate database for each salesperson. Each database would contain summary sales data for the stores serviced by a particular salesperson. The IS staff have indicated that they are able to provide the data that Ms. Andrews has in mind in the form of database files in ACCESS format.

Ms. Andrews asks you to work with the IS department to get a set of sample data for a single salesperson and use that data to build a prototype of this application system. She specifically asks that your prototype application produce a report sorted by store and summarizing recent data about sales, stockage, past dated units (packages not sold by their suspension date), a computation of the daily sales rate for each store over each sales period, and a computation of the inventory turnover rate (units stocked / daily sales rate) for each store over each sales period.

Upon consultation with the IS department you are provided with a small sample of data for one salesperson covering a one month time period. A few records of this data are shown below and this set of sample data is available on your data disk in an ACCESS database called **Case65_PbL.mdb**. If you are using a database package other than ACCESS you will need to use the import operation to retrieve this table of data into your database.

Sample Sales and Stockage Data

Sales_Stock						
SLSP NO	STORE NAME	SALES DATE	ELAPSED TIME	UNITS SOLD	UNITS STOCKED	UNITS Suspended
M7602	Jones' #46	10/22/2004	7	280	350	
M7602	Fresh - N - Rite #17	10/22/2004	6	209	380	27
M7602	Jones' #48	10/23/2004	7	325	325	
M7602	Econo Bag	10/23/2004	10	178	300	34
M7602	Vin's Supr Mart #7	10/24/2004	8	343	400	
M7602	Vin's Supr Mart #9	10/24/2004	8	350	350	

Note that the number of days since the last previous sales visit has been computed from the organizational database and is included in this file. Based on this data, the daily sales rate for a store can be computed as units sold divided by the number of days since the previous visit. Once the daily sales rate is known, the inventory turnover rate can be calculated by dividing the units stocked by the daily sales rate. For example, for the first record, average daily sales are 280 divided by 7 or 40 packages per day. Based on that figure, the inventory turnover rate can be calculated as 350 divided by 40 or 8.75 days.

Application Development Notes

Since a database file specifying the structure of the data and providing a sample set of records for this case has been provided, you should examine the structure of this table as you begin to design your application. An appropriate set of analysis and design documents should be created for this case. Then, using these documents and the data provided proceed to create a reporting system to produce the required reports.

Assignment

1. Based on the description above and the database file provided, generate an appropriate set of analysis and design aids for this application. Using these aids, develop a database application meeting all the requirements of this case. Test your application for accuracy and completeness.

2. Create a set of presentation materials summarizing the key features of your application and describing the procedures required to operate and maintain it. Be sure that your materials include full coverage of appropriate control and back-up procedures.

3. Based on the sample data, can you see stockage adjustments that need to be made? Write a brief report summarizing adjustments to stockage levels that you would propose based upon the sample data. Attach copies of the reports you generated and use them to justify your proposed stockage adjustments.

CASE 6: Pit Stop Rentals

The Pit Stop is a convenience store located in a small resort area. Because of its remote location, the Pit Stop stocks not only convenience foods, but also a variety of hardware and houseware items. Eve Davis, owner of the Pit Stop, has always attempted to expand the services her shop offers in response to changing markets.

Last year, Eve began offering DVD rentals. Memberships are available at no charge to area residents. Eve has about 150 members of her video club and maintains an inventory of about 200 movies. Until now, she has maintained all video club records in manual form. She has purchased a personal computer and would like to automate much of her record keeping, beginning with her video rental operations.

Eve has assigned each club member a unique three digit member ID number. Eve has an index card for each membership showing the member ID number, the member's name, address, and phone number, and a list of names of additional family members who are permitted to rent movies under this membership. This set of index cards is sorted alphabetically by the last name of the member in a box with tabs for each letter, so that she can quickly verify the identity of a customer.

Eve also keeps a set of index cards describing her inventory of movies. The information she maintains for each movie lists the movie's title, the category of the movie (Children's, Action, Western, Drama, Comedy), the movie's rating (G, PG, or R), and a unique four character ID code that Eve assigns to each movie when it is received. Samples of the cards Eve uses are shown below.

Rentals are made strictly on a cash basis. That is, each customer pays a one-day rental fee for the videos she/he rents at the time of the rental. All movies are due to be returned by six o'clock of the evening following the date on which they are rented. Movies returned late are subject to an appropriate additional fee which is collected at the time that they are returned. When a movie is rented, the rental date is written, in pencil, on that movie's index card. The index card for the movie is then placed behind the card of the member checking it out. When a movie is returned, the date on the card is checked and a late fee is charged if appropriate. Then the date is erased and the movie card is returned to its file.

Customer Index Card

CUSTOMER ID#: *073*

CUSTOMER NAME: *Joe Davis*

ADDRESS: *348 Lark Lane*

PHONE #: *4-2843*

Movie Index Card

MOVIE ID#: *A028*

MOVIE TITLE: *The Matrix*

CATEGORY: *Adventure*

RATING: *R*

DATE RENTED: *10/16/04*

Eve plans to computerize her entire movie rental operation. She wants to develop a computerized system to track her inventory of movies and her list of members. As a part of her inventory tracking, she wants to keep track of the status of each movie - is it in the store or is it checked out to some customer. At this point, she is not interested in keeping a rental history for each movie she only wants to know whether it is currently checked out and, if so, who checked it out and on what date did they check it out?

Eve has asked you to develop an application for her that will store information about her inventory of movie videos and allow her to retrieve summary information about them. Eve wants your application to provide a report listing of movies by category. This report should show the ID number, title, and rating for each movie and be grouped by category and would be provided to customers to help them select movies.

Another report that Eve wants is one that lists all movies that have been out for more than one day. This list would show the name and title of the movie, the customer ID number, name and phone number of the customer who rented it, and the date of the rental. This list would be used to assess late fees and to call customers who may have forgotten to return the movies they rented.

Eve has prepared the set of sample data shown below for your use. This sample reflects the current status of selected movies in Eve's inventory and information about a selected set of customers. For the movies that are rented, Eve has added the ID number of the member who checked them out since she wants this data to be available in her database.

Application Development Notes

Your first step in developing the application for this case should be to perform analysis and design activities and generate an appropriate set of analysis and design aids for use in implementing your application. The design and creation of a database table structure is an important part of this case. Based on the description above, the sample data shown, and the entity relationship diagram below, you should create tables with the appropriate structure. Next, you should create forms for entering and maintaining movie and customer data. Then you will need to enter the sample data shown below. Finally, you should create the report or reports and queries needed to meet the output requirements of this application.

ENTITY RELATIONSHIP DIAGRAM

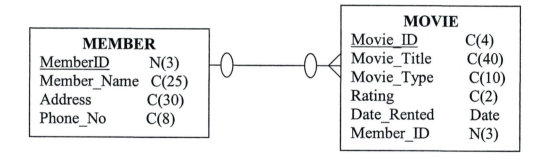

Member

Member ID	Member Name	Address	Phone No
6	Al David	304 Oak Trail	3-1762
24	Lance Bates	409 Lakeview Lane	3-1973
42	Sue Morris	106 Oak Trail	3-2061
46	Ned Gaultt	146 Lark Dr.	4-2391
52	Dean Ellis	206 Lucky Lane	4-1924
58	Nolan Reynolds	214 Lark Dr.	4-2752
73	Zoe Eavis	348 Lucky Lane	4-2843

Movie

Movie ID	Movie Title	Movie Type	Rating	Date Rented	Member ID
A015	The African Queen	Drama	G		
A019	Galaxy Quest	Comedy	PG	10/17/2004	6
A023	Fantasia	Children's	G		
A024	Pearl Harbor	Drama	PG	10/17/2004	24
A028	The Matrix	Adventure	R	10/16/2004	58
A029	The Rocketeer	Adventure	PG	10/16/2004	58
A043	Barbershop	Comedy	PG	10/15/2004	46
A064	Hard Times	Comedy	G	10/16/2004	42
B003	Notorious	Drama	PG	10/17/2004	24
B006	Return of the Jedi	Adventure	PG	10/17/2004	52
B024	Dances with Wolves	Western	PG		
B026	Shane	Western	G	10/17/2004	73
B027	The Matrix Reloaded	Adventure	R		
B031	The Graduate	Drama	PG		
B041	Fight Club	Drama	R		
C002	Dr. Strangelove	Comedy	PG		
C014	The Unforgiven	Western	R	10/17/2004	52
C017	The Princess Diary	Children's	G		
C042	The Shootist	Western	PG	10/17/2004	73

Assignment

1. Based on the description above and the sample data shown, design a full set of analysis and design aids for this application. Using these aids, develop a database application meeting all the requirements of this case. Test your application for accuracy and completeness. Print the two reports produced by your application.

2. Write an appropriate set of documentation to accompany your application. Be sure that your documentation fully describes all of the procedures that Eve will need to follow including appropriate back-up procedures.

3. Create queries to answer each of the following example customer questions:
   a. "Is The Unforgiven checked out currently and if so, when is it due to be returned."

b. "I'm Ned Gault. Can you tell me if there are any movies currently checked out to my account?"

c. "I'm looking for an adventure movie that is not R rated. What movies do you have available that meet that description?"

CASE 7: Flexi-Staff

Flexi-Staff is a temporary employment agency specializing in workers with clerical and secretarial skills. Flexi-Staff operates in a town with a population of about 25,000 located in the Southeastern United States. Flexi-Staff places workers in temporary jobs whose duration ranges from a few hours to two weeks. Workers wishing to be employed can sign up with Flexi-Staff by coming in and filling out a form. No fee is charged to the workers. Companies pay a fee to Flexi-Staff and the workers are employed by, and paid by, Flexi-Staff. Hiring companies can receive a list of available workers with the skills they need. Alternatively, the prospective employer can request that Flexi-Staff select a worker for them. In the former case, the employer selects the worker they want and then informs Flexi-Staff of whom they selected. In the latter case, the staff of Flexi-Staff contacts qualified workers until they find one who is available for the requested job.

Flexi-Staff contracts with an outside firm to handle the processing of billing and payroll. Operating in this way, Flexi-Staff has not required any computerized systems. Thus far, all data about the workers has been kept on index cards. As each job comes, in the cards are searched to find potential qualified workers. There are substantial problems with this method of record keeping. First, searching records manually is very awkward and time consuming. Secondly, it is difficult to keep track of how often a particular worker is offered employment. There have been numerous complaints that some workers were called for jobs much less frequently than others "with the same sets of skills." Finally, the manual system simply is not capable of handling the volume of workers and jobs that Flexi-Staff is currently experiencing.

Flexi-Staff is about to begin its third year of operation. Jane Goodwin is the founder and owner of Flexi-Staff. She feels that the manual system for tracking workers and allocating jobs is at a crisis point. One of her highest priorities is to computerize the data about workers and jobs. She wants to maintain this system internally and to keep it independent of the billing and payroll systems. Flexi-Staff has a PC with database software available for this purpose. Jane has asked you to develop this application.

Jane is able to supply you with a sample of the index cards used to record worker information. One of these cards is shown below.

Sample Worker Index Card

```
NAME:    Ann Carnes
PHONE#:  638-2174

AVAILABLE FOR WEEKEND WORK:          Yes

JOBS/SKILLS:                         Skill Level

        Typing:                          2
        Dictation:                       1
        Word Processing:                 3
        Spreadsheet                      2
```

As a worker signs up, they are asked to indicate their skill level, with respect to a number of common office skills. Skills are designed as 1, 2, or 3 for low, medium, or high. If a worker has no skill in a particular area, they leave that item blank. Jane allows each worker to self report their skill level, but she indicates that she may suspend a worker from future jobs if there are complaints that the worker's skills were not up to the level required. Thus far, Jane has had little trouble with workers whose skill levels were less than they reported. Workers also are asked to indicate whether or not they are available for weekend work. Jane has found that some employers need workers for weekend work on emergency projects and that some of her workers are unable or unwilling to work at those times. Jane feels that this set of information is adequate to screen her workers for prospective jobs.

Jane has used set of index cards to store information about jobs as well. A sample is shown below. It essentially asks for a contact name and phone number for the job, asks what skills are required for the job and whether weekend work will be required, and indicates the starting and completion date of the job. A sequential job ID is created for each job, and the name of the employee assigned to the job is added once that information has been determined. Currently each job can have only one worker assigned. If an employer seeks more than one worker, Jane creates multiple job cards with different ID numbers so that there is only one worker associated with any job ID. Jane indicates that she wishes to keep this structure in the computerized system since it is rare that someone calls wanting multiple workers with the same set of skills.

Sample Job Index Card

```
NAME:    Lee Davis
PHONE#:  4-8136
WEEKEND WORK REQUIRED:            No

JOBS/SKILLS REQUIRED:                    Skill Level

    Typing:                              2
    Dictation:
    Word Processing:                     2
    Spreadsheet:                         1

JOB START DATE:               09/14/04
JOB COMPLETION DATE:          09/22/04

WORKER ASSIGNED:
```

Jane is concerned about the fairness of her system for allocating workers to jobs. She wants to have a system that will ensure that all workers have equal opportunity to secure jobs for which they qualify. Toward this end, she suggests that a contact date be stored in the database. This date would be updated each time a worker is contacted about a job opportunity. Jane is hoping that this date can be used to sort the list of qualified workers retrieved for any job assignment, so that those who have gone the longest since the last job opportunity will be placed at the top of the list and contacted first. Once a qualified worker is contacted about a job this "contact date" would be updated whether or not they took the job. However, when a prospective employer requests a list of available workers, only the worker selected will have the contact date on their record updated. This is because Flexi-Staff has no way of knowing which of the workers on the prospect list were actually contacted.

Under the manual index card system, the cards of workers placed in jobs were pulled from the active file and placed in a file of unavailable workers organized by the concluding date of the job assignment. At the end of each day, the cards for workers whose jobs were scheduled to end on the current day were returned to the active file. Jane indicates that your application will need to do "something of this nature." That is, you will need to know which workers are assigned to jobs that are not yet completed and will have to ensure that those workers are not included in lists of prospective workers for jobs with overlapping dates. Jane suggests that this might be accomplished by storing the completion date for a job in the record for the worker who is assigned to that job.

Completion dates later than the current date would prevent a workers record from being retrieved. This date would simply be written over when a new job is assigned to a worker.

The application you create should be able to produce a report listing the names and phone numbers of workers available for a particular job. The user should be able to simply enter the job number of a job and have a report listing all available workers qualifying for this job. This report should be sorted on "contact date" so that the worker with the least recent contact will be placed at the top of the list. To be "available" for a job a worker must not have a current job whose completion date overlaps with the proposed job. Also they must have the skills needed to complete the proposed job and, must willing to work weekends if the proposed job requires weekend work. This report will be used by Flexi-Staff to assign workers to a job or sent to employers who wish to do their own screening.

Jane also wants to be able to link the job and worker data to produce a report displaying the job number, the contact's name and phone number, the assigned worker's name and phone number, and the completion date for all current jobs (jobs with an assigned worker whose completion date is after the current date). Jane also indicates that she would like to be able to produce a report, for any worker who requests it, summarizing information about all of the jobs to which that worker has been assigned.

A number of employees at Flexi-Staff will be retrieving listings of available workers, entering data records for new workers who have just signed up or new jobs that have been received, and updating the records when workers are contacted and/or accepted for new job assignments. Jane herself will handle an ad-hoc querying of the system, making of back-up copies of the database, and correction of mistakes. Jane Goodwin has an intermediate level of skill in the use of database packages. However, many of her employees have no previous computing experience.

To help you get a feel for the data involved, Jane has been able to provide you with the sample set of data below. These data are for your use in developing and testing the application. She has even included a set of hypothetical contact and job completion dates for your use.

Sample Worker Data

Worker ID	Worker Name	Wkr Phone	Work Wkends	Dicta-tion	Word proc	Spread-sheet	Contact Date	Job Compl Date
2	Jen Jones	8-2762	No	B			9/17/2004	9/6/2004
5	Ed Flynn	4-8297	No	B	B	A	9/14/2004	9/7/2004
7	Ann Barnes	8-2174	No		B	B	9/16/2004	9/3/2004
8	Brad Case	6-2868	Yes		B		9/16/2004	9/20/2004
11	Stan Mann	4-8326	Yes		C	A	9/14/2004	9/11/2004
13	Alice Ames	5-8392	Yes	C	B	B	9/10/2004	9/5/2004
14	Ben Barnes	6-0927	No		B	B	9/12/2004	9/1/2004
16	Pat Carnes	8-2174	Yes	C	A	B	9/15/2004	9/22/2004
17	Della Eads	8-2132	Yes	C	C		9/17/2004	9/18/2004
19	Jim Jones	4-8274	Yes		B	C	9/17/2004	9/6/2004
20	Eve Smith	4-6284	Yes	B	C	C	9/12/2004	9/2/2004
21	Sue Taylor	7-8273	Yes	C	B		9/12/2004	9/3/2004
22	Gale Boyd	6-8629	Yes		B	B	9/11/2004	9/20/2004
23	Pam Powers	7-1037	No		C	B	9/10/2004	
24	Lynn Cline	6-8273	Yes	C	B		9/13/2004	9/23/2004

Sample of Job Data

Job ID	Contact Name	Contact Phone	Wkend Work	Dicta-tion	Word proc	Spread-sheet	Start Date	End Date	Worker ID
121	Ann Smith	3-7819	No	C	A		8/28/2004	9/4/2004	2
128	Lee Davis	4-8136	Yes		B		9/5/2004	9/6/2004	19
133	Jack Dahl	4-2973	No		B		9/12/2004	9/22/2004	16
137	Ali Grant	7-2193	No	B			9/2/2004	9/10/2004	8
142	Lynn Bush	3-2851	Yes		C	C	9/3/2004	9/8/2004	11
155	Sue Smith	5-1890	Yes			B	9/4/2004	9/6/2004	2
162	Ann Taws	7-9105	No		C	C	9/3/2004	9/10/2004	22
167	Dan Price	4-2867	Yes	B	C		9/5/2004	9/18/2004	17
176	Ed Vance	3-9217	No		B		9/6/2004	9/10/2004	24
181	Dee Morris	2-6193	Yes		B		9/17/2004	9/20/2004	8
183	Eve Cole	5-7623	No		B	B	9/12/2004	9/20/2004	22
188	Jan Jones	6-6832	Yes		B		9/13/2004	9/23/2004	24
196	Lori Lewis	4-2817	No			A	9/20/2004	9/25/2004	
204	Tom Piper	7-8213	Yes	B			9/21/2004	9/21/2004	

Application Development Notes

Before beginning to implement your application for this case, you should develop an appropriate set of analysis and design aids. The creation of a database table structure is an important part of this case. Based on the sample data shown and the entity relationship diagram below, you should create the appropriate table structure. After creating the tables you will need to enter and verify the sample data that are provided. You will create three reports. A report of workers available for a particular job, a report summarizing all pending jobs, and a report of summary information about all jobs assigned to a particular worker. The structure for each of these reports is quite simple. However, the query used to determine the set of workers available for a job is complex. You will want to test the selection criteria very carefully.

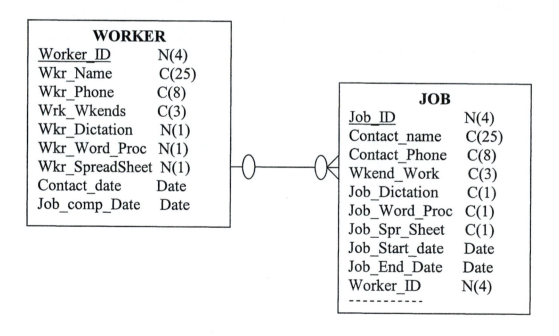

WORKER

Worker_ID	N(4)
Wkr_Name	C(25)
Wkr_Phone	C(8)
Wrk_Wkends	C(3)
Wkr_Dictation	N(1)
Wkr_Word_Proc	N(1)
Wkr_SpreadSheet	N(1)
Contact_date	Date
Job_comp_Date	Date

JOB

Job_ID	N(4)
Contact_name	C(25)
Contact_Phone	C(8)
Wkend_Work	C(3)
Job_Dictation	C(1)
Job_Word_Proc	C(1)
Job_Spr_Sheet	C(1)
Job_Start_date	Date
Job_End_Date	Date
Worker_ID	N(4)

Assignment

1. Based on the description above and the sample data shown, generate an appropriate set of analysis and design aids for this application. Using these aids, develop a database application meeting all of the requirements of this case. Test your application for accuracy and completeness.

2. Prepare a set of presentation materials appropriate for presenting you application to Jane and her staff. Your materials should highlight key findings and describe the procedures Jane and her staff will need to use.

3. Write an appropriate set of documentation to accompany your application. Be sure that your documentation fully describes all of the procedures that Jane and her staff need to follow. Procedures should be described in a level of detail that is matched to the needs of the different users of the system. You should also be sure that your procedures include complete descriptions of control and back-up procedures to be used.

4. There are likely to be numerous instances where querying of your database will be required. To demonstrate that your database can handle queries, retrieve the following data from your database.
   A. A count of the number of jobs requiring evening work.
   B. A count of the number of workers possessing at least some skills in each of the skill categories.
   C. A listing of all jobs whose completion date is after 10/22/98 which have a worker assigned to them.

5. Suppose that Flexi-Temps starts allowing a single job to have more than one worker assigned. Further assume that Flexi-Temps wants to begin tracking its employer customers to identify repeat business. How would the table structure of the database need to change to capture these characteristics? Draw an entity relationship diagram showing what the modified database would look like.

CASE 8: Midwest Restaurant Supply

NOTE: This case is based upon the same situation described in spreadsheet Case 6. This case is designed to show that many applications can be developed using either spreadsheet or database software.

Midwest Restaurant Supply is a wholesaler of restaurant supplies and equipment. Midwest began as a supplier of coffee and coffee making equipment to restaurants. Over the years, Midwest's business has expanded to include a wide variety of nonperishable, expendable restaurant supplies and all types of restaurant equipment.

The sales staff at Midwest Restaurant Supply are paid primarily on a commission basis. They receive a modest base salary that is adjusted once a year and a commission whose amount is calculated monthly based on three components. A percentage commission is paid on sales of supplies, a different and higher percentage commission is paid on sales of equipment, and a bonus amount is paid for each new customer found by a salesperson. *Currently these rates are 1.5% on supplies, 2.5% on equipment and $50 per new customer.*

Commission rates are set by the Vice President of Marketing, Jan Jones. Ms. Jones likes to make adjustments to the commission rate structure occasionally to provide appropriate incentives. For instance, if equipment sales are slow and equipment inventory is up, she may temporarily raise the commission percentage for equipment. Similarly, if she feels that the sales staff has not found enough new customers lately she may raise the bonus for new customers. When adjustments to the commission structure are made, they are effective at the beginning of the next calendar month.

Because of the complexity and changing nature of the commission system used, commissions have always been hand-calculated. Midwest's uses a PC based accounting software package to handle its order processing and billing. That package is used to produce a monthly summary listing of sales of supplies, and sales of equipment for each salesperson. Each salesperson submits a list of new customers they have attracted that month. This list is verified from the accounting data to determine the count of new customers.

Ms. Jones has requested that you create a computer application to store this monthly listing and produce a report showing the amount of commission and bonus, as well as, the total gross pay owed to each salesperson. She would also like to have summary information, such as, totals for salary, sales of supplies, sales of equipment, number of new customers, and commissions paid. There are no current plans to produce reports based upon data from prior months. However, Ms. Jones does want to retain each month's data in an accessible form for possible future uses.

Jan Jones indicates that she has no experience with the use of computers and plans to turn the application over to her assistant, Alden Everett. Alden has experience using word processing software on the computer but is a novice in the use of spreadsheet and database software.

A sample set of data for this table covering the months of August and September 2004 is provided to you on your data disk. This set of data is available in an ACCESS file called **case68_mrs.mdb**. Two tables are used for this application. A Salesperson table stores the name, ID number, and Salary of each salesperson. Since the amount of sales changes each month and we want to keep a record of each month's sales, a Monthly_Sales table is used to store the sales data for each salesperson each month. Samples of the data in these tables are shown below.

Sample of Data

MONTHLY SALES

SLSP ID	Sales Month	Supplies	Equipment	NEW CUST
103	8/1/2004	$64,889.00	$56,120.00	6
104	8/1/2004	$49,319.00	$57,240.00	1
105	8/1/2004	$55,085.00	$45,344.00	5
106	8/1/2004	$60,068.00	$71,416.00	3
107	8/1/2004	$67,589.00	$53,344.00	6
108	8/1/2004	$55,593.50	$56,059.20	4

SALESPERSON

SLSP ID	Salesperson Name	Monthly Salary
103	Moran, Sue	$575.00
104	Murray, Ben	$500.00
105	Peterson, Pamela	$575.00
106	Sanders, Arnold	$550.00
107	Garland, John	$625.00
108	Franklin, Jim	$475.00
109	Elston, Ed	$525.00

Application Development Notes

Since tables specifying the structure of the data for this case have been provided, you should examine the structure of these tables as you begin to design your application. An appropriate set of analysis and design documents should be created for this case. Then, using these documents and the data provided, you will proceed to create a database report to produce the required summary information. Calculation of the commission earned by each salesperson can be done through a query which permits the user to enter values for the commission parameters each time the query is run.

Assignment

1. Based on the description above and the database file provided, generate an appropriate set of analysis and design aids for this application. Using these aids, develop a database application meeting all the requirements of this case. Test your application for accuracy and completeness.

2. Create a set of presentation materials highlighting key features of your application and describing the procedures that will be required to operate and maintain it. The materials you develop should be appropriate for a presentation to Jan Jones and Alden Everett.

3. Write an appropriate set of documentation to accompany your application. Be sure that your documentation fully describes all of the procedures Alden needs to

follow including appropriate back-up procedures.

4. There are likely to be numerous instances where querying of your database will be required. To demonstrate that your database can handle queries, retrieve the following data from your database.
   A. Retrieve a list of the names of all Salespersons who attracted at least 3 new customers last month.
   B. Retrieve a list of the names of all salesperson whose sales of Priority Items were greater than average sales of priority items last month.

5. Write a brief discussion paper addressing the following questions:
   A. What are the advantages and disadvantages of using a database package as opposed to a spreadsheet package for this application?
   B. Could you build an application using your database software package that would allow you to keep track of cumulative "year-to-date" commissions earned by salespersons? Note that, to do this, your application would have to record the amount of commission earned by each salesman each month in the database and would need to allow commission rates to be modified without changing the value of commissions earned in previous months. Describe how you would modify your application to accomplish this task.

CASE 9: Pace Picnic Products

Pace Picnic Products is a small scale manufacturer of plastic products. Pace produces plastic picnic supplies including plates, cups, tablecloths, and knives, forks, and spoons. The majority of Pace's sales are of disposable supplies. However, Pace also produces a line of heavy duty plastic picnic supplies designed for repeated use and this has been Pace's fastest growing product line in recent years.

Pace's products are all produced at a single factory in the Southeast. At this factory there are a number of production lines. Distinct and different production lines are used for the manufacture of tablecloths, plates, cups, and utensils. The utensil production lines can produce any type of utensil: knife, fork, or spoon. Also, any of the production lines can be shifted from producing the lighter, disposable line, to producing the heavy duty, reusable, line of products. The production lines at Pace Picnic Products normally run 2 shifts a day 5 days a week.

Changes to machinery required to switch production from one type of utensil to another, or from light duty to heavy duty products, are time consuming. For that reason, production runs are planned so that each line produces a particular product through an entire work week. Changes required to produce a different utensil or weight of product are made while the plant is shut down over the weekend.

In order to keep up with demand, Pace occasionally uses overtime and operates its production lines one or two hours longer. On those occasions each shift is given the same amount of overtime work. The day shift comes to work two hours earlier and the evening shift stays two hours later.

Mel Wells is the Director of Product Testing at Pace Plastic Products. His staff gathers samples of the output of each production line several times during each shift and tests the samples for quality and strength. At the end of each shift the number of units tested and the number of defective units found on each line are recorded. Mel's staff also records the total output of each production line for each shift. This information is kept in manual form until the end of the week. At the completion of each week, the production and inspection information for each shift on each production line is summed across the days of the week to produce a weekly Production and Quality Report which is transmitted to the IS Department and recorded in computerized form. An example of this form is shown below.

Production and Quality Report

PRODUCTION WEEK 23

Line	Product	Shift	Hours	Output	Units Tested	Defective Units
A1	Fork	Day	42	93470	986	17
A1	Fork	Eve.	42	79211	1031	15
B2	Knife	Day	40	123071	954	22
.	.	.		.	.	.
.	.	.		.	.	.
.	.	.		.		
C3	Spoon	Eve.	40	63411	805	16

Data are recorded in the organizational database only on a weekly basis because, until recently, the inspections were performed much less frequently and product pulled from several days of production on a line was often pooled into a single inspection group. Thus, it was impossible to produce meaningful daily inspection data for each shift and line. Since the inspection data can now be meaningfully recorded on a daily basis, Mel Wells and the shift foremen would like to have daily shift performance information available in computerized form.

Mel submitted a proposal to Pace's IS Steering Committee for the conversion of this system to a daily recording and reporting basis. Because of a substantial applications backlog, the IS Steering Committee has adopted a policy of encouraging end user development of applications. When they reviewed Mel's proposal they indicated that the IS Department would not be able to perform this conversion for at least 18 months. However, they suggested that Mel consider end user development of his application.

Mel Wells has asked you to develop a prototype of this application for him. He indicates that the application should record production level and inspection results for each line in computerized form immediately at the end of each shift. The application should generate the Weekly Production and Quality Report that is submitted to the IS

Department. This will cut down on employee time spent computing weekly totals and eliminate manual computation errors.

Beyond this routine output, Mel would like your application to be able to produce a report at the end of each week which would compare production on a given production line across shifts and days of the week. Because different lines produce products with different expected levels of output and defect rates, one weekly report of this type would be produced for each line and no comparisons across lines would be used. Mel would like this report to include a calculation of the average output and average defect rate across the entire production week, where the defect rate for a given shift-day is simply the percentage of tested units that are defective. Mel also wants the report to include comparisons of each shift-day's performance to those averages. In other words, this report should compute the average of output and the defect rate across all shifts and days of the week and add a column comparing the levels for each particular shift-day to those averages. The comparisons to average would then be expressed in percentage terms. Thus, if average output per shift-day is 12,000 units and the output for the evening shift on Tuesday is 12,600, then production for the Tuesday evening shift is 105% of average.

Mel provides you with the set of sample data shown below for your use in developing a prototype of this application. He indicates that when the application becomes operational the inspectors on each shift will enter their shifts data each day, but that he will personally operate the application to produce the outputs he has described. Mel Wells is an experienced user of PC spreadsheets and database software, but many of his inspectors have no prior computing experience.

Application Development Notes

Your first step in developing the application for this case should be to perform analysis and design activities and generate an appropriate set of analysis and design aids for use in implementing your application. The design and creation of a database table structure is an important part of this case. Based upon the description above and the sample data shown, you should develop a data dictionary form for these data and use its specification in creating your database table. Once your table structure has been created, you will need to enter the sample data shown above. Data will need to be sorted by shift for each of the reports in this application. The Weekly Production and Quality Report can be generated as a summary database report. However, data for each production line across all shifts and days of the week should be copied into a spreadsheet file for production of the report comparing each shift and day to average production levels and defect rates, since comparisons to average are not directly supported by most PC database packages.

Production and Inspection Data							
Line	Product	Prod_Week	Day	Shift	Output	Units_Tested	Defective_Units
A1	Fork	23	1-Mon	Day	13007	183	4
A1	Fork	23	1-Mon	Eve	13017	185	3
C3	Spoon	23	1-Mon	Eve	8701	184	4
C3	Spoon	23	1-Mon	Day	7659	162	1
B2	Knife	23	1-Mon	Day	17799	175	8
B2	Knife	23	1-Mon	Eve	18323	179	4
C3	Spoon	23	2-Tue	Eve	7742	164	8
C3	Spoon	23	2-Tue	Day	8755	198	4
A1	Fork	23	2-Tue	Eve	12110	178	6
A1	Fork	23	2-Tue	Day	13701	182	2
B2	Knife	23	2-Tue	Eve	18573	186	4
B2	Knife	23	2-Tue	Day	19103	203	2
B2	Knife	23	3-Wed	Eve	18252	185	8
A1	Fork	23	3-Wed	Day	12733	185	2
C3	Spoon	23	3-Wed	Eve	7887	178	5
A1	Fork	23	3-Wed	Eve	13051	173	6
B2	Knife	23	3-Wed	Day	20662	196	5
C3	Spoon	23	3-Wed	Day	7486	156	4
A1	Fork	23	4-Thu	Day	13135	189	5
A1	Fork	23	4-Thu	Eve	12094	170	6
B2	Knife	23	4-Thu	Eve	18643	183	3
C3	Spoon	23	4-Thu	Day	8451	176	2
C3	Spoon	23	4-Thu	Eve	8308	185	1
B2	Knife	23	4-Thu	Day	19367	190	1
B2	Knife	23	5-Fri	Day	19519	181	1
B2	Knife	23	5-Fri	Eve	17810	176	3
A1	Fork	23	5-Fri	Day	13761	202	4
C3	Spoon	23	5-Fri	Day	8837	199	4
C3	Spoon	23	5-Fri	Eve	7809	164	6
A1	Fork	23	5-Fri	Eve	13206	193	1

Assignment

1. Based on the description above and the database file provided, generate an appropriate set of analysis and design aids for this application. Using these aids, develop a database application meeting all the requirements of this case. Test your application for accuracy and completeness.

2. Write an appropriate set of documentation to accompany your application. Be sure that your documentation fully describes all of the procedures needed to operate this application including appropriate control and back-up procedures.

3. Do you think that this is an appropriate application for end user development? Does this application create important organizational data that could be useful to a variety of individuals within the organization? Could this application be extended and eventually be incorporated into an organizational database? Write a brief discussion paper assessing these issues.